# Business
# Development

# Business Development

A guide to small business strategy

## David Butler

OXFORD   AUCKLAND   BOSTON   JOHANNESBURG   MELBOURNE   NEW DELHI

Butterworth-Heinemann
Linacre House, Jordan Hill, Oxford OX2 8DP
225 Wildwood Avenue, Woburn, MA 01801-2041
A division of Reed Educational and Professional Publishing Ltd

A member of the Reed Elsevier plc group

First published 2001

**British Library Cataloguing in Publication Data**
Butler, David
    Business development: a guide to small business strategy
    1.   Strategic planning   2.   Small business
    I.   Title
    658.4'012

ISBN 0 7506 5247 0

For information on all Butterworth-Heinemann publications visit our website
at www.bh.com

Typeset by Florence Production Ltd, Stoodleigh, Devon
Printed and bound in Great Britain by Biddles Ltd
*www.biddles.co.uk*

FOR EVERY TITLE THAT WE PUBLISH, BUTTERWORTH-HEINEMANN
WILL PAY FOR BTCV TO PLANT AND CARE FOR A TREE.

# Contents
Contents

Contents

## Contents

# Preface
Preface

Preface

This book is aimed primarily at owner-managers of small businesses, who having hopefully survived the early traumas of starting or acquiring the business and then frequently struggling to reach a level of relative stability, can now pause for breath, and ask themselves the question – where do I go from here?

Its predecessor *Business Planning – A Guide to Business Start-Up* was aimed first and foremost at those people who are considering going into business or self-employment. It also linked to the NVQ3 Business Planning qualification, which is based on the Small Firms Enterprise Development Initiative National Vocational Standards for Business Planning, which were revised in 1999 and published in summer 2000. In a similar fashion, this book is aimed both at small businesses which are in their early stages of development and at the training qualifications which are available for owner-managers in that position. In this case, the book focuses on the SFEDI National Vocational Standards for Business Development. These were also revised in 1999 for publication in autumn 2000, and lead to the NVQ4 Owner-Manager qualification, or the Institute of Management Certificate in Owner-Management.

Great! But what busy owner-manager in their right mind has time to spare to leave their business to chase after a qualification that proves they can do what they are already doing? The answer to this is relatively few, which is why the NVQ4 qualification has had a fairly low uptake compared with its level 3 counterpart. Let's face it, if you have to produce a business plan for the bank manager in order to start your business then there is some justification in using that to achieve a qualification at the same time. But a year or two down the line priorities will have changed, and it is the business itself rather than the gaining of additional qualifications which is first and foremost in the owner-manager's mind. This is particularly true as most formal qualifications require substantial commitment in terms of time and effort. The owner-manager's time is usually under great pressure, and it is the business itself which is the main focus for effort and energy.

Many established owner-managers also find that what they primarily need are more concise or compact training opportunities which focus on specific areas of need, and this is where the revised standards will come into their own in the future.

For the past ten years, support for small firms has often been an uncoordinated, if not haphazard process, with substantial local variance in the extent and quality of provision. The local enterprise agencies have been the first-stop source of advice for business start-up and early years support, although the latter has increasingly become the realm of the local Business Links. Training advice has been the responsibility of the Training and Enterprise Councils (TECs), which in some areas are one and the same as the Business Links. Some TECs have sought to co-ordinate local training provision with local colleges and private training providers, whilst elsewhere other TECs have sought to place these in competition with each other. Funding for training has been available from TEC budgets, the Further Education Funding Council (FEFC), local education authority Adult Education budgets, and grants from local authorities. At long last the government has proposed a solution to the confusion, with TEC and FEFC funding being combined under the local Learning and Skills Councils from 2001, and with the establishment of the Small Business Service, which will replace the TECs and Business Links with local franchises. Those franchises will cover areas which will be concomitant with the Learning and Skills Council areas, and are intended to provide a more co-ordinated and cost-effective support service for small businesses.

A major opportunity arising from these changes is to offer the Business Development Standards for a new range of small qualifications based around clusters of related NVQ Units, e.g. marketing or finance. By using them as free-standing qualifications rather than full NVQs, owner-managers can target their own specific development needs. Small firms can already access funding for training to help them gain Investors in People status, and it is hoped that LSC funding will become available to support these clusters. SFEDI have also designed the Standards for use by small firms as a yardstick to improve their business performance without necessarily being linked to formal training. This book aims to provide practical and useful ideas for owner-managers, whether they are studying for a full formal qualification, a cluster of Units to develop their skills in a specific business area, or simply wanting to improve their performance to grow their businesses.

Small businesses are often accused of being unable to think strategically, or of failing to plan for the long-term future. The structure of this book is aimed at following a logical sequence of questions to facilitate that process. It starts by asking the questions: 'Where are we now?' – the strategic analysis of the business and its operating environment; and 'Where do we want to go?' – the process of defining strategic objectives. It follows on with more tactical issues: 'What resources will be needed to get there?' and 'What sales and marketing policies will we need to develop?' It asks whether overseas exports are appropriate to the business and how these could be developed. It examines the personnel and staffing implications of the foregoing activities, and the efficiency and effectiveness of current financial management processes. It then looks at the overall financial implications of the strategy and how they will be met. Finally, it looks at the way the whole strategy will be implemented to achieve the planned objectives.

David Butler

# Acknowledgements
Acknowledgements
Acknowledgements

To my wife, for her patience and support and to my son, for bailing me out every time the computer crashed.

To Dr Pete Newman (wilderness-solutions.com) for his advice on Internet marketing and for providing invaluable case study material based on his own business.

# Chapter 1 The culture shift

Chapter 1
Chapter 1

**The social and economic context**

Throughout the second half of the twentieth century, the vast majority of management training and theory was focused on the big-company model, and more specifically on big manufacturing companies. However, in the last two decades of the century a social change started – often described as the post-modernist movement – when the society formerly dominated by institutionalized systems and governments and large organizational employers began to be replaced with a more personalized culture – 'the empowerment of the individual'. It is no accident that this evolution followed the post-war increase in materialism and increased consumer spending power and personal mobility, and that it coincided with major changes in telecommunications and information technology. At the time, the pundits were all forecasting shorter working hours and increased leisure time for the working population; however, the biggest impact of high-powered technology was on manufacturing industry, where expensive skilled manual labour was rapidly replaced by automated and computerized manufacturing systems. As a result, the pundits were proven wrong, with a large part of the working population becoming unemployed whilst others were working increasingly long hours in the hope of maintaining their employability. The same process was going on in the public sector, with downsized levels of operation due to the cost savings arising from new technology, and the enforcement of competitive tendering in local authorities and the National Health Service.

One of the biggest outcomes of these socio-economic changes was that the idea of self-employment or owner-management was no longer the doyen of local shopkeepers, family businesses and tradesmen. Up to then, although self-employed tradesmen were generally regarded as respectable members of society (apart perhaps from some in the second-hand motor trade!), there was still the element or association of self-employment as being a 'working class' activity rather than a proper 'professional' career. Fortunately, the technological revolution also swept away much of the ethos of defined social class structures and the stereotyped job-types that went along with them even up to the 1960s. Self-employment rapidly gained renewed respectability and attraction, particularly amongst recently unemployed skilled workers with new-found wealth resulting from substantial redundancy payments. The reduced size of public sector direct-labour organizations and the introduction of competitive tendering also generated many opportunities for new small businesses to spring up in the service sectors. The IT industry itself was focused on continual rapid change and growth, which were again incompatible with the old traditional patterns of employment-for-life. It needed a much more flexible workforce capable of working on short-term contracts in flexible multi-disciplinary teams. Furthermore, the IT industry was willing to pay high fees for such flexibility that could best be provided by self-employed professionals on a contractual basis.

As a result of all of these changes, and the new-found respectability of self-employment, the late 1980s and early 1990s saw a boom in the number of self-employed people and new small businesses. Inevitably, a significant proportion of these were destined to fail, but such was the scale of start-ups and failures, and the enthusiasm for owner-management, that there was no longer a social stigma associated with bankruptcy or insolvency resulting from 'having a go on your own'. Former bankrupts are no longer regarded as social lepers – they are just regarded as people who tried but did not quite make it. In many cases, they received a great deal of public sympathy for their treatment by the high street lending banks, who had at times made finance too easily available, only to pull the carpet from under their feet when the going became tough. The lending banks have also received a great deal of criticism in recent years for systematically exploiting the vulnerable position of small firms with punitive account charges and rates of interest. Big companies simply would not stand for it, but the small firms do not have the power or influence to challenge the banks, and are often vulnerable because of their dependency on the banks for day-to-day support when cash is tight.

## The political context

As early as 1971, the British government had shown a little interest in the structure of small businesses when the Bolton Committee Report (1971) attempted, rather haphazardly, to define the sizes of small firms across a number of key industries. For example, a 'small' manufacturing firm had less than 200 staff, whereas 'small' mines and quarries had only twenty-five or less. In the motor trade, a 'small' firm had a turnover of under £100k, but in the wholesale trade the turnover was £200k, 'small' transport firms had less than five vehicles, and catering businesses were small so long as they were not multiple outlets or brewery-managed. With such vague definitions it was not surprising that the government had no clear or positive policies towards small firms, although the New Enterprise Programme of the 1970s was the first, albeit unsatisfactory, attempt to support small firms by encouraging training and development.

It was only in the mid-1980s that the true importance of the small firms sector began to attract real government attention as larger organizations began to shed staff. As a result, the small firms sector emerged as the potential alternative to the large employers, and an alternative which could help to reduce the politically sensitive high and rising levels of unemployment. It was the solution to the big threat which could lose the controlling party the next election. Various initiatives and support mechanisms were developed to assist small firms to start up

3

and to grow, including the DTI Enterprise Initiative, and the Business Growth Training Option of the early 1990s.

In 1998, the Department of Trade and Industry estimated that there were 3.75 million small firms providing 7.7 million jobs, and that of all UK firms, 84 per cent had less than ten staff and 89 per cent had less than five staff. This broadly correlates with the Small Firms Lead Body (now the Small Firms Enterprise Development Initiative) figures from 1998, stating that 96 per cent of all UK firms employ less than twenty staff. This implies that the big companies, whose needs dominate the content of management training provision throughout the UK, constitute only 1–2 per cent of the total number of employer organizations in the UK.

One problem that still persists is the insistence of the government in using the term 'SME'. The DTI defines a Small or Medium-sized Enterprise as having less than 250 employees or an annual turnover below £5 million. Unfortunately, there is a continuing and confusing implication within this definition that prompts the assumption that the needs of a new small firm with just five to ten staff are the same as a firm employing 200 staff that has been established for twenty or thirty years. With the current high value of new technology, a very small firm with just a handful of staff can be involved in high-value contracts exceeding £5 million, whilst another much larger business employing substantial numbers of unskilled staff on low-paid labour intensive work can have a turnover below that figure. In this context, annual sales turnover has become largely irrelevant, and it would make much more sense to sub-divide the sector, for example, into micro firms (with under twenty full-time equivalent staff), small firms (with twenty to fifty full-time equivalent staff) and medium-sized firms (having fifty to 100 staff). In effect, most firms with 100 to 250 staff are relatively large and well established these days, and certainly tend to employ the necessary specialist management skills that are usually found in larger companies. The difference in size also becomes critical in more rural counties, where there are significantly fewer businesses in the 100 to 250 employee bracket, but a great deal more micro firms which form the bulk of potential local employment. On this basis, the current government definitions certainly need to be reviewed to focus support funding into the parts of the small firms sector which is likely to produce the most long-term growth and potential employment – which the government continuously tells us are the newly established and nursery businesses. It is these to which the following chapters will apply most.

**The training and education context**

The provision of management and business training really started to expand in the 1970s, primarily through the poly-technics and some of the more technically focused UK universities (it was then still not quite a respectable academic subject at that time – except of course at Harvard). This provision has expanded over the years, both upwards to postgraduate level at most universities and downwards through colleges of further education. One of the key problems, however, is that the majority of the demand for such training is on a part-time basis, e.g. where employees are given day-release from work to attend college, or by distance learning through the Open University or similar institutions. The major drawback is that historically this type of education or training does not attract the same levels of funding as full-time education, and as a consequence students are normally charged quite substantial course fees, which in the vast majority of cases are paid for by their employers.

In a survey of part-time business and management students carried out at South Kent College during 1997 and 1998, less than 5 per cent came from small firms, and the majority (75 per cent) of that group were paying their own fees as their employers would not or could not afford to sponsor them. If, as is suggested above, the remaining 95 per cent of students on these courses are derived from the 1–2 per cent of large employer organizations whose training needs dominate the management education provision in the UK, then clearly there is a major imbalance and lack of proper direction in management training provision. In simple terms, there is a substantial and almost critical need for business and management training in the small business sector, but central funding for this within the further and higher educational system is not readily available. Those who need it most can least afford to pay for it, and the educational funding systems are not designed to facilitate the provision of the sort of short, flexible, convenient training programmes that small firms need because they are invariably not qualification-related! I know this to be true from my own experience of trying to develop new training programmes for small businesses. (Okay, that's my soapbox preaching contribution over with, so now we can move on.)

The predominance of students from large companies on management programmes has inevitably resulted in those programmes being directed towards the needs and interests of large organizations, with little or usually no reference to the needs or interests of their smaller counterparts. Corporate Planning, Public Sector Finance and International Marketing are great subject options for employees of large organizations, but the big-company model of management training is woefully inadequate for the owner-manager, and it is only in very recent years that this problem has started to be redressed. In the mid-1990s there were only a handful of UK universities offering small-business programmes or options (Durham and Warwick being two examples also notable for their SME-related research), but the number is now steadily growing.

Not only is the large organization model inappropriate for business and management training, it fails to acknowledge the fundamental cultural differences between large and small organizations:

## The owner-manager culture

- Large organizations can afford to employ specialists to provide particular management or administrative functions, e.g. personnel, payroll, sales, marketing, purchasing, distribution, accounts, etc. The owner-manager generally has, at least in the formative years of the business, to fulfil the majority of these roles without specialist support. In the small firm, the emphasis is on breadth of knowledge and skills, in contrast to the specialist expertise and knowledge available in large organizations.

- Medium-sized and large organizations tend to produce Corporate Plans specifying their aims and objectives over a three- to five-year period. These 'strategic' plans are produced at senior or board level, and are implemented by middle managers at the 'tactical' level. Below them, the middle managers have junior managers or supervisors to whom the day-to-day 'operational' decisions are made. In contrast, in the small firm, strategic thinking or planning rarely takes place in the early stages of its development (see Table 1.1).

- Until a small firm has reached a level of stability, the whole of its existence is a matter of survival, and consequently its focus is on the short-term measures that will enable it to achieve survival. Long-term or strategic planning is non-existent, and in truth is often irrelevant – after all, what is the point in planning for next year if the business may have to close next month? Whereas large firms can afford to invest in staff development and training, this will only happen in small firms, and particularly the newer ones, where that training will offer a short-term payback for the time and effort invested, e.g. a very rapid increase in sales, or substantial cost savings. Similarly, if the owner of a small firm takes time off, or sends a member of staff for training, it is highly unlikely that anyone will be available to cover for the absence. Lost time is lost revenue for the owner-manager, so compared with the big-company counterpart, the actual cost to the business of sending staff away for training is much more critical, as it results in the loss of a higher percentage proportion of revenue income. Conversely, however, it can be argued that as a matter of survival, the small firm owner cannot afford not to invest in training if that training provides the skills to survive. This is the Philistine view that if they do not take the trouble to arm themselves with the basic skills and knowledge to survive in business, then they do not deserve to survive anyway! I wonder how people who hold such views handle the concept of customer care?

- Owner-managers, in particular those who have previously been employed as managers, tend to be fiercely independent and often reluctant to take advice, which may be fine if they actually have the necessary skills and expertise to establish a business. However, unlike the situation in large firms, when they hit problems there is often no one to consult or to provide expert advice. Again, the tendency in such circumstances is to opt for the most immediate practical solution, or the cheapest short-term solution, perhaps to the detriment of the longer term needs of the business.

- The finances available from lending banks and financial institutions tend to be much more restricted than for big companies. Interest rates tend to be higher, and the sums offered are frequently lower in proportion to the equity required to secure them. True, this is not a problem for well-established and profitable small businesses, but the financial system, as it stands, makes the achievement of that condition much harder to achieve anyway. New small firms simply do not have any negotiating power when it comes to interest rates and terms of borrowing.

- The political, legal and fiscal environment in which small firms operate is constantly changing, and in recent years has resulted in an ever-growing burden of bureaucracy. Whilst big companies may have the resources (if not the inclination) to handle these burdens, the pressure put on small firms is disproportionate to their size, turnover and profitability. Unpaid tax collection responsibilities (VAT and PAYE, etc.) in particular impose a disproportionate burden on smaller firms. In spite of frequent government pledges to reduce red-tape, the burden continues to grow, largely due to our association with the European Community and its central-control culture. If only Scott Adams were to venture into the EU headquarters in Brussels and Strasbourg, I am sure he would find an everlasting supply of material for his Dilbert cartoon strip! Come to think of it, doesn't Dogbert sometimes wear a French beret?

## Key phases of small business development

From my observations and experience as an owner-manager and in training and advising other owner-managers over the past few years, I have observed a three-phase pattern of small business development. This is by no means a universal model but it does help to understand the development process. In some cases, new firms fold or their owners withdraw or give up before even reaching the end of the first phase, and in others the business is only started when an established and growing market is already in place – effectively skipping straight to the third phase. Some others with less ambitious objectives simply decide to stop at the second phase. However, I would estimate that the vast majority – say 80 per cent or more – move through these phases during their development. A summary of the three phases is shown in Table 1.1.

### Phase 1 – Business start-up

In the initial start-up phase of a new small business, the emphasis is primarily on survival and the struggle to reach break-even level and profitability before the limited working capital runs out. Typically, this phase will last between six months and three years, although in extreme cases some small firms will struggle on for five years or more before reaching stability. The entrepreneur's personal objectives are focused on reducing personal financial exposure – especially if the family home has been offered as security against borrowing – but there is also

*Table 1.1* **Development stages for the majority of small firms**

| Development Phase | Duration | Primary Business Objectives | Entrepreneur's Personal Objectives | Typical Behavioural Characteristics | Decision Making Processes |
|---|---|---|---|---|---|
| START-UP | 6 months to 3 years | – Survival of the business<br>– To reach break-even level before working capital runs out | – To achieve profitability at the earliest opportunity to reduce personal financial exposure<br>– Sense of achievement / personal satisfaction | – Accept all available business<br>– Focus on gaining extra marginal contribution to costs rather than overall profitability<br>– Tendency towards headless-chicken syndrome: much activity and effort generating relatively low profit margins | – Primarily operational<br>– Tendency for tactical decisions to be subsumed by chance of marginal contribution<br>– Focus on short-term returns with little strategic thinking |
| RELATIVE STABILITY | 1–2 years | – Consolidation<br>– Review and revise the operational processes of the business | – To increase profit to ensure the long-term survival and stability of the business (and to reduce personal financial risk in the process)<br>– Move towards achieving return on capital investment, and repay personal effort. | – Consolidation of activities, more focus on profitability/ profit margins<br>– More selective attitude to customers e.g. rejection of slow payers and low-profit business<br>– More attention to customer needs, quality and long-term relationships<br>– Tendency to stagnation and complacency in some firms if this phase lasts too long | – Switch from operational to tactical thinking<br>– Initially not much strategic thinking, but this increases towards the end of the phase as a basic pre-requisite of the next phase |
| GROWTH and DEVELOP-MENT | On-going in future years | – Planned expansion to increase market share, turnover and profit<br>– Capital growth | – Expand market share and sales turnover to generate and increase personal wealth<br>– Continue the reduction of personal financial risk (less urgent now)<br>– Expand personal power and influence | – Confidence and stability achieved in the second phase provides the basis for a more adventurous attitude towards the marketplace<br>– Future growth financed from profits, and external funding now more readily available<br>– Importation or development of more specialist management skills, and increased delegation of responsibility | – Primarily strategic and tactical<br>– Operational decisions tend to be increasingly delegated as business grows |

the desire for a sense of achievement or accomplishment. The tendency during the first phase is to accept any business which offers even the smallest contribution to overhead costs and profit. This marginal approach can often result in the owner-managers and staff running around like headless chickens in the pursuit of marginal contributions to profit, resulting in a deleterious affect on profit margins (and the owner-managers ending up totally knackered – its no joke, I have seen it more than a few times!). What is essentially happening is that management decisions are being made at a purely operational level on the basis of short-term returns, and with little or no strategic thinking. Then as the owner-managers have no staff to delegate the marginal work to, they end up working extra, and relatively unproductive hours, doing the work themselves, to the neglect of the overall management of the business. We call this the headless chicken syndrome.

## Phase 2 – Relative stability

Once a new small firm has consistently achieved a level of trading above that of the break-even level for a few months, a sense of relief occurs with the owner-managers. A major hurdle has been jumped, and there is now the opportunity for a period of stability and consolidation within the business. Typically, this phase will last between one and two years, by which time most spirited entrepreneurs will be looking to further growth. The key features of this stage involve the review at operational level of the processes of the business. The owner-manager is concerned with improving profitability, reducing operating costs and waste, and is now, for the first time, in a position to make decisions about which customers to retain, and which (e.g. the bad or slow payers) to relinquish.

The emphasis is now less on survival and more on the increase of profit and the reduction in personal financial exposure. The owner-manager is looking for a return on capital invested plus a premium for the personal effort which has been put into the

11

business. As a result, there is much more focus on profitability and the maintenance of healthy profit margins, coupled with a more selective attitude towards customers. This heralds the first opportunity to say 'No, I don't want or need your business or the aggravation associated with it' – at last slow or bad payers can be rejected in favour of good steady customers, or low-profit work can be turned down. There is also a focus on customer needs to ensure the long-term retention of regular customers, and along with this goes a positive effort to improve standards of quality within the business.

Unfortunately for some small firms, this stage becomes their primary objective, and in some cases a sense of complacency ensues. I am not saying that there is anything wrong with not wishing to expand a business beyond a basic level of comfort, but for most modern cultures there is a desire to push beyond this stage. It is also argued that in a constantly changing technological and economic environment, no business can afford to stand still without the risk of losing its place in the market. I would think, however, that at the bottom end of the SME spectrum there are many micro firms and self-employed individuals who simply do not wish to continue expanding, particularly if they are personally financially stable.

What really characterizes the second phase is the progressive switch from operational to tactical thinking. There is still not a great deal of strategic thinking involved, but as the desire to expand becomes more predominant, then the switch to strategic thinking must occur as an essential prerequisite of the next phase – basically, without ambition and forward thinking the next phase will not be achieved.

## Phase 3 – Growth and development

This is an ongoing process for future years, involving a planned expansion to increase market share, sales turnover and profit. Apart from expansion, the other key objective will usually be that of the capital growth of the business. Both the owner-manager and the business (which by now may be a corporate entity) are looking for an expansion of market share and increased profits, and a consequent expansion of their personal power and influence. The entrepreneur's personal financial risk is less of an issue at this stage. The overall confidence achieved from the second phase provides for a more adventurous attitude to the marketplace – what other markets exist that have not yet been exploited? There is also much less financial pressure on the business as funds for future development are becoming available. Typically, the recognition of the need for change in management practices to facilitate future growth results in increased levels of delegation. This is the one fundamental factor without which future expansion cannot proceed, and this is usually accompanied by the importation or development of new and additional management and staff skills, giving the opportunity for improved systems of delegation. At this level, decisions are primarily strategic and tactical, with operational decisions being increasingly delegated to supervisory levels of management as the business grows.

## The culture shift

This is the essential change in small business culture and owner-manager attitude that is the prerequisite to the future growth and development of the business. Essentially it is necessary for the entrepreneur to make a positive shift from just making tactical decisions and day-to-day operational decisions, into a proactive higher gear which will involve strategic planning for the future of the business. Unfortunately, this is one of the hardest moves which owner-managers are faced with, as it involves relinquishing many of the 'comfort-factor' management responsibilities which have evolved alongside them during the early days of the business. In the infamous Video Arts training video 'The Unorganized Manager', John Cleese, playing St Peter the custodian of the Pearly Gates, described this as the process of 'growing up'. Invariably it involves delegating some of the control and responsibility previously associated with the early growth of the business, which because

13

of those associations can often be a painful process. For example: 'I *want* to keep maintaining the sales ledger to keep in touch with the business revenue' – irrespective of the fact that an accounts clerk can do the job in half the time, with better accuracy, and at a significantly lower hourly rate! And while the manager is dabbling with the sales ledger, who makes the strategic decisions – are they left to the accounts clerk or do they just get postponed until he has some spare time?

It is very easy for owner-managers to underestimate the effects their own personalities have on their businesses and in particular on the staff they employ. The fact that they occupy such a singularly dominant and influential role within the business means that the culture that operates within the business inevitably tends to reflect their own attitudes and personalities. In turn, that reflection is projected to the outside contacts, the customers and suppliers. An aggressive and autocratic style can often evoke a defensive attitude or blame culture amongst the staff, and conversely, a caring and democratic style can generate a positive and congenial attitude in staff. Such attitudes and cultures are more than visible to any outsiders who come into contact with the business, and naturally, many of those outsiders are customers. Part of the culture shift therefore involves the owner-managers in becoming aware of the impact their own personalities have on the firm, and in ensuring that the impact does not have a negative influence.

The key to future growth and expansion requires a basic change in attitude and thinking – a veritable cultural shift – by owner-managers. It is the transition from direct involvement in all aspects of the operational control of the business, to a position and attitude of more senior management responsibility, wherein the operational aspects are delegated to allow more time to focus on the strategic planning and development of the business. By working through the various stages of the strategic planning process shown in Figure 1.1, the owner-manager can make the necessary culture shift to improve the performance

## The strategic planning process

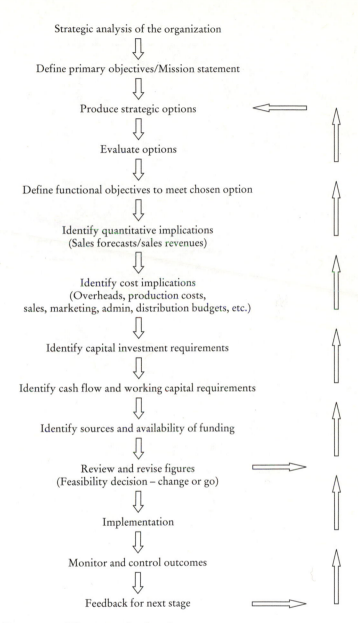

Strategic analysis of the organization

⇓

Define primary objectives/Mission statement

⇓

Produce strategic options

⇓

Evaluate options

⇓

Define functional objectives to meet chosen option

⇓

Identify quantitative implications
(Sales forecasts/sales revenues)

⇓

Identify cost implications
(Overheads, production costs,
sales, marketing, admin, distribution budgets, etc.)

⇓

Identify capital investment requirements

⇓

Identify cash flow and working capital requirements

⇓

Identify sources and availability of funding

⇓

Review and revise figures
(Feasibility decision – change or go)

⇓

Implementation

⇓

Monitor and control outcomes

⇓

Feedback for next stage

*Figure 1.1*   The strategic planning process

## Strategic Units

A1 Review the business
A2 Develop your plans for the business
A3 Check your own management skills
B1 Plan how to improve your sales and marketing
B3 Explore markets abroad
B4 Plan how to develop the business using the Internet
D1 Carry out your business plan
D3 Make changes to improve the business
D4 Take key decisions that will affect the business
G1 Plan how to improve the finances of the business
G3 Get finance for the business
J1 Review you staffing

## Tactical Units

B2 Improve your sales and marketing
B5 Sell products and services to customers
C1 Look after your customers
C2 Improve your service to customers
D2 Improve the quality of your products and services
E1 Get the right premises for the business
E2 Improve your use of equipment, tools and materials
F1 Develop a website for the business
F2 Communicate using IT
G2 Make the most of finances in the business
G4 Get customers to pay more quickly
L2 Conduct an assessment of risks in the workplaces

## Operational Units

B6 Negotiate sales
B7 Prepare and present sales proposals and quotations
C3 Solve customer's problems with the services given the business
C4 Improve relationships with your customers
F3 Choose and use computers and software
H1 Improve your time management and delegations skills
J2 Deal with poor performance and handle staff complaints
J3 Move staff to new roles or make them redundant
J4 Recruit staff
K1 Make sure your staff can do their work
K2 Get the right services or supplies from another business
K3 Help your staff to learn
K4 Coach your staff
L1 Control risks to health and safety

*Figure 1.2* Breakdown of Revised Business Development Standards

and focus on the direction in which the business is to go. Following this process does not imply total loss of contact with the operational side of the business. It should rather be seen as a move to optimize management resources to improve the tactical and operational performance of the business.

## The Revised Business Development Standards

So, having identified the need for the culture shift – the reincarnation of the owner-manager as a strategic thinker – just where do the Revised SFEDI Business Development Standards fit into the picture? They were essentially conceived as standards of performance to which a competent owner-manager of a small business should be capable of achieving on a consistent and regular basis. In doing so, he or she would be operating what are best described as systems of good practice within the business, at strategic, tactical and operational levels. Figure 1.2 shows how the Revised Standards broadly break down within those three levels.

In addition to providing the framework for the NVQ4 in Business Development or similar qualifications, the revised SFEDI standards are capable of underpinning a whole range of development activities, whether formal or informal. They can be used to support short courses or skills development activities that focus on particular business functions such as exporting, sales and marketing, manpower planning, resources management and finance. But equally they can provide a structure against which the working owner-manager can examine and monitor the performance of his or her business on an ongoing basis, on an operational, tactical or strategic level.

There is already an abundance of good textbooks and written material relating to the operational aspects encapsulated within those Standards, e.g. staff supervision, effective presentation skills, dealing with customers, mentoring staff, health and safety, etc., all of which are relevant to large and small businesses alike. Therefore, the ensuing chapters will focus on the more strategic and tactical aspects of the Standards and how these relate to small and evolving businesses in particular.

## Reference

Bolton Committee (1971). *Report of the Committee of Inquiry on Small Firms*. HMSO.

## Further reading

Hall, G. (1995). *Surviving and Prospering in the Small Business Sector*. Routledge.
Institute of Management (1996). *Developing Managers in Smaller Firms*. IM.
Kirby, D. (1990). Management education and small firms development, an exploratory study of small firms in the UK. *Journal of Small Business Management*, 28, Oct. 1990.
Storey, D. J. (1994). *Understanding the Small Business Sector*. Routledge.

# Chapter 2  Performance review – where are we now?

Chapter 2
Chapter 2

The purpose of this chapter is to describe the processes which can be used to analyse the past and current performance of a business – the where-are-we-now scenario. In effect, this is the first stage of the quantum leap from operational to strategic thinking. The process will enable us systematically to examine and critically review the key aspects of business performance, and to identify areas where actions are needed to improve or strengthen current systems and procedures. This goes beyond an analysis of the strengths and weaknesses of the business, and the opportunities and threats it faces – that was okay for the start-up stages of the business but now we need to examine the needs of the business in more detail. It is, in effect, an audit of each facet of the business and the way it operates. It attempts to answer the first of the three key questions asked by the strategic planning process – where are we now, where do we want to go and how do we get there? The chapter also relates to the three mandatory Units within the Revised Business Development Standards – A1: Review the business; A2: Develop your plans for the business; and A3: Check your own management skills.

Lasher (1999, p. 8) makes the distinction between Corporate Strategy as the process which takes place in large organizations to optimize the performance of their diverse activities, and Competitive Strategy which takes place in smaller companies, or larger ones in single lines of business activity. There are a number of well-established strategic analysis models that can be used for performance review, although they are primarily designed for use in that big-company corporate strategy context. For example, the McKinsey 7S analysis, which examines the business in terms of its Structure, Systems, Style, Staff, Skills, Strategy and Shared Values – picture six circles in a rose pattern with the seventh (the Shared Values) in the centre of them.

- The Structure represents the formal organization of the business, lines of authority and responsibility, and the resources at its disposal, how the organization breaks down its activities into distinct elements and how those elements are co-ordinated.

- The Systems are the formal and informal communications, processes and procedures that link the various parts within the structure to each other to facilitate co-ordination and control.

- Style is concerned with the way the managers operate within the business, the philosophies, values and beliefs adopted by them in exercising their authority and achieving results.

- The Staff are the human resources within the business, the quantity and quality of the people employed.

- The Skills are the competencies (both available and required) in order to perform the various tasks to a sufficiently high standard.

- The Strategy of the organization is the summary of its key objectives and activities, and long-term policies. It includes the actions (proactive) and reactions (reactive) to developments in the external environment, e.g. the route to profitability or success.

- The Shared Values are the aspects of organizational culture which are common to the various parts of the organization and which overlap with each of the other six. They are the values (written or unwritten) which underlie the stated objectives of the organization and which *should* be shared by all of its members. These are often referred to as the 'super-co-ordinate goals', e.g. ethics, standards of performance and behaviour, attitude to quality.

The McKinsey 7S framework can be useful in helping with identifying and understanding how the business operates, but it is really better suited to larger organizations where the functional departments are more remote from each other. In a small business this is rarely the case, although the 7S headings may assist the owner-manager to describe and comprehend how his or her own business works.

The Johnson and Scholes (1997) model of strategic planning employs the three key stages of Strategic Analysis, Strategic Choice and Strategic Implementation.

- The Strategic Analysis examines the Environment in which the business operates by auditing the environmental influences on the organization. It further analyses the Expectations, Objectives and Power – the organizational structure, culture, management style and its ability to implement its objectives. Finally, it looks at the Resources at its disposal (physical financial and people resources) and how they are balanced to contribute towards the strategic capability of the organization, i.e. how it will be able to sustain its policies in the future.

- The Strategic Choice is concerned with generating and evaluating the strategic options available to the organization, and selecting the appropriate strategy for the future needs of the organization, e.g. maintain the status quo, go for expansion, develop new products or export markets, or to diversify the range of products and services offered by the business.

- The Strategic Implementation looks at the three key areas of planning and allocating the resources, the organizational structure, and the people and systems; how these

21

factors must be changed and developed enable the Strategic Choice (the chosen option) to be implemented successfully.

It is interesting that Johnson and Scholes point to one of the major obstacles that inhibits successful Strategic Planning as the tendency of big-company managers to focus too much on their own functional areas (production, finance, marketing, etc.) whilst failing to take a more holistic overview of the business. In theory, this ought to be one area where owner-managers score highly by virtue of the need for them to be competent in a broad range of management skills to run the business, particularly in the earlier stages of its existence. However, as discussed in the previous chapter, the various pressures and stresses of running a small firm usually contrive to keep the owner-manager thinking at the operational and tactical levels, and rarely having time to aspire to the holistic or strategic perspective. In practice, the owner-managers of small firms and the functional managers of big organizations both need to be kicked into strategic gear, but in the case of the small firm it is only the owner-managers themselves (or occasionally their spouses or bank managers) who are in the position to do the kicking!

The big drawback with big-company models such as these is that they cannot always be easily applied or related to the small business situation. This is simply because of the nature of this nefarious beast 'the owner-manager', whose role of jack-of-all-trades and sole decision-maker is incongruous alongside the big-company model wherein that role is spread across a range of specialist experts who all congregate and contrive to contribute towards the decision-making processes. Mintzberg (1994) suggests that 'Effective strategists are not people who abstract themselves from the daily detail, but quite the opposite: they are the ones who immerse themselves in it while being able to abstract the strategic messages from it'. There can be no doubt that owner-managers are good at immersing themselves in their businesses; the hard part is getting them to take a step backwards to be able to see the strategic messages.

## The organizational environment

Before we can consider expanding the business we need to ensure that the various aspects of the business are operating efficiently, or at least as well as they can within existing financial constraints and management abilities. The process of performance review involves analysing in detail the organizational environment in which the business operates, as shown in Figure 2.1. That is, the internal environment within the organization itself, the trading status of the business, its finances, physical resources, staff and management skills, operational and control systems, policies and procedures, stakeholders' interests, etc. These are essentially factors which are, or should be, within the control of the business. The market environment in which the business operates is an area over which the owner-managers have some influence but not control, e.g. the customers, suppliers, competitors, media, etc. The external envi-

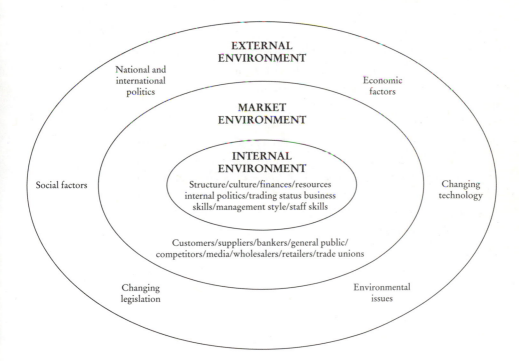

*Figure 2.1*   The organizational environment

ronment consists of factors which are outside of the control or influence of the business, but which can still have a major impact on the way in which it operates, e.g. changes in legislation, social and political policy, economic trends, etc.

The analysis involves finding answers to a whole range of detailed questions relating to the management and operation of the business under these three headings. By working through the questions, we should also be able to identify necessary changes that must be undertaken in order to create the right conditions for further development of the business.

### The trading status of the business

What is the current trading status of the business – sole trader, partnership, co-operative or limited company? Is this satisfactory at present? Is it likely to be satisfactory for future needs? If not, what alternative options exist that might meet the needs of the business? For example, a sole trader or partnership that has been operating successfully in a small local wholesaling business, but now wishes to expand, may need to reconsider its status. If the expansion is to be substantial, e.g. opening new branches or substantially increasing the number of credit customers, this could leave the owners vulnerable to substantial exposure and risk from bad debts in the future. Limited liability status might reduce the extent of the exposure, although it might also reduce the borrowing capacity of the owners unless they are willing to offer personal assets as security against borrowing. The trading status may also be affected by interpersonal factors, e.g. partners who wish to develop the business in differing directions. Alternatively, it may be that a sole trader is looking to take a partner on board to inject capital into the business, or to assist with its expansion and development by increasing production capacity.

*The internal environment – within the business itself*

## The management skills within the business

The capacity of the business for future expansion is usually thought of in terms of available finance and the ability to expand the markets. However, even if these factors are available, the future expansion can still be inhibited by deficits in other management skills – staff management and leadership, financial planning and control, operations management, and information management. Therefore, before we look at expansion, we need to know the current position in terms of management capabilities. What business and management skills or knowledge currently exist within the business? Are these being used to the full? Are these sufficient for the current needs of the business? Are they likely to be adequate for the future needs of the business or will other skills need to be imported or developed? What are the particular skills that are lacking? Are there any staff within the business who could be trained in these skills? What would be the cost of training in terms of money and productive time lost from the business? Is suitable training available? Is training viable or would it be easier to recruit skilled staff or to buy-in the necessary skills from an external provider? Can we afford to buy in the skills? What would be the cost and operational implications of not having the necessary skills, i.e. can we afford not to have them?

## Current policies and the decision-making processes

The current policies within the firm may not even be specified or written down, as with relatively young firms these tend to evolve as the business establishes itself and starts to grow. As explained in Table 1.1, these will also be initially influenced by the simple need to survive and to reach break-even level before the working capital is exhausted. Only after that stage is reached can proper forward planning begin. So, what exactly are the policies or strategies currently being utilized? Initially, they are likely to relate to maximizing sales and revenue, and subsequently to improve the profit margins within the sales

25

revenue, and the marketing policy will tend to follow these rather than to lead to new opportunities. In fact, as we have discussed in the previous chapter, in the early months of the business the owners will tend to employ tactics as opposed to strategies. In a similar vein, the decision-making processes will have been reactive rather than proactive. Ask yourself the questions then: what do I currently want from my business and am I achieving that? What key decisions have I made that have helped me to achieve my objectives and how were those made? Who else did I involve in the process? Were they spur of the moment decisions or carefully considered? What bad decisions have I made and what were the consequences? What mistakes have I made? How can I avoid repeating them? The reflective process may be uncomfortable or even painful to face up to, but it can be most valuable in planning for the future.

## Stakeholders' interests and objectives

Who are the stakeholders in the business? Most obviously the owners or shareholders who have invested in the business and have risked their personal assets, but also the providers of loan capital whose repayment will depend on its success. The employees are also dependent on it for continued work and their own families for the income, the suppliers for continued custom, and the customers for a reliable source of goods or services. (Not forgetting the Chancellor for all the unpaid tax collection that small firms do on his behalf!) There may well be others that you can identify. What do these stakeholders think or your achievements so far? Are they satisfied with your performance? Have you met their expectations or let them down? Your own family or dependants are also stakeholders – what do they think of your enterprise, and has it met with their expectations both in terms of the business and you as a person? The direct families of owner-managers can easily become the most neglected of stakeholders as business demands take priority over the needs of the family.

**The financial resources, capitalization, working capital and cost structure**

First, we need to examine the capitalization – is the business funded predominantly by equity, long-term borrowing, from reserves generated by previous years' profits or a combination of these? What is the current borrowing capacity of the business, and is adequate security available to support further borrowing? Does the company need to consider selling shares in the business to raise more capital? Second, there is the question of working capital – is it adequate for current needs, or are we relying on overdraft facilities and credit from our suppliers? Is the working capital adequate to allow for planned growth without further borrowing, or would we run the risk of over-trading? Third, how do our operating costs compare with those of our rivals in terms of higher or lower overheads, variable production costs (can we buy components cheaper than them?) and profit margins. Are these acceptable and sustainable in the long term?

**The financial systems**

These are the controls and record systems currently used within the business, and rarely have they been designed specifically for the operational requirements of the small firm. They tend to have evolved on a needs basis, with extra bits being bolted on as the business changes or expands, or as more demands for financial information are requested by lenders or the company auditors. In terms of financial records they will include sales, purchase, nominal ledgers, sales invoicing, customer statements and accounts, payroll and PAYE returns, VAT records, petty cash payments and receipts, etc. The main questions are, how efficient and time consuming are these to operate, and do they give us the information we need when we need it? In terms of financial controls we are looking at the monitoring of cash flow, collecting debts on time, paying our suppliers on time, and controlling and reconciling cash and bank figures with the ledger system. Are we managing our cash flow efficiently or having to use valuable time chasing debts to enable us to pay the bills? Do our customers keep within agreed credit terms or do we allow these to slip? Do we tend to stretch our suppliers' credit to the absolute limit? Is this adversely affecting our relationships with the suppliers? In terms of financial planning, do we regularly monitor our sales and expenditure figures against planned budgets to identify variances and potential problems, or do we just react to the crises when they hit us?

## Past financial performance and profitability

In an ever-changing business environment, past records of profitability and performance may not be directly relevant to the current trading position, especially if the business has turned the corner from loss-making to a position of steady profit. The accounting records are the tangible evidence that the business and its managers have (hopefully) shown a trend of progressive growth and profitability that would justify the interest of a potential lender or investor, and answer the key questions. Has the business made a regular profit in the past? If not, what are the reasons for this, or the main barriers to profitability? What has happened to make us believe that this will change in the future? The past performance may not necessarily relate to what is happening within the business right now, particularly with relatively young businesses, so we must ask: is the business trading profitably at present, and is it likely to start trading profitably and to continue to do so in the future? Which business activities generate the most profit and which generate the least? Bearing in mind that even low profit sales still contribute towards overhead costs, can we justify any changes to these activities, or should we concentrate on high profit margin activities? Are our profit margins above or below the industrial average, or those of our competitors, and do we know why this should be the case? If they are lower than average, are the current profit levels still acceptable to the owners or stakeholders in the business? It may be the case that the owners rate long-term stability and survival above maximizing short-term profits, or that they are still in the process of gaining a foothold in the market and are currently working on reduced margins. The emphasis here should be on understanding the reasons behind past performance to help plan future policies.

## Monitoring and control systems

These will be largely determined by the nature of the products or services which the business is offering. In a manufacturing output they will relate to control of materials usage, standard costs, production outputs, product quality, etc., whereas in a wholesale or retail operation they may involve stock ordering and rotation, meeting delivery deadlines, and achieving sales volumes. In service industries, there may be more emphasis on customer care and retention, and minimizing complaints. The questions arising then are – what monitoring and control systems do I currently have in place, and do they work? Is the information generated by them of practical use to me? Is the information up to date? What other data do I need to make my business work better? Are there any gaps in the present systems, perhaps highlighted by recurrent problems? What changes could be made to make the current systems more efficient and cost-effective?

## The staff resources and their deployment

If done properly, the review of staff skills can be a lengthy but useful process. First, who are the staff and management, what are their roles in terms of their job descriptions, and what do they really do? Are any of them under-utilized, or could they be better deployed elsewhere in the business? Do any of them have skills or expertise not currently being used to the full? Do we actually need them all, or do we in fact need to employ more staff to improve our efficiency? In an ideal world, the business would have two matrices – one of the range of technical and business skills needed to operate the business efficiently and profitably, and the other covering the staff employed and the respective skills they can offer. Unfortunately, owner-managers do not live in ideal worlds, and these matrices tend to be luxuries found in bigger firms who can afford to employ specialist training and personnel staff. In the real world, the value of a member of staff tends to be noticed most when they are sick or on holiday, and either you do not miss them at all or you are desperate for their return.

## The physical location and premises

Premises are an expensive overhead and often a long-term commitment, and if they are in the wrong place, or are too small, or are used inefficiently, they can become a major drain on the profits of the business. So, where are the premises currently located? Are they sufficiently close or convenient to the customers or markets supplied by the business? If the business is involved in physical deliveries, are the premises located conveniently close to major road or rail networks? Are they adequate in terms of size, or do they currently restrict the capacity of the business? Is this because they are too small or because they are not being used efficiently? How much are they costing us at present? Will the premises be adequate to accommodate possible future expansion? Are alternative suitable premises available? These are the main issues that must be considered in the review of the current business performance, but they will also have implications for future planning. What would be the cost of moving premises and the associated costs of disruption to production and customers? Would these costs be justified by the extra potential capacity for production or storage? Should we consider renting, leasing or buying alternative premises? How would the additional overhead costs affect the profitability of the business? Can we afford to move to new premises? Again, can we afford not to make the move if we wish to expand and grow?

## Physical resources, plant and equipment

When planning a new business the potential entrepreneurs are usually advised to produce an inventory of physical resources which inevitably includes all of the ideal equipment and materials, but which is abruptly revised once costs are identified. The second attempt usually divides the list into essential items and those which can be acquired as and when funds permit. How far down the line have you gone with these? Do you now have a full inventory of plant and equipment covering all items that are regularly used? Do you have an active policy of maintenance and replacement or do you just buy new items when the old ones are beyond repair? Are you making full productive use of your inventory or is machinery sitting idle and costing you money for the space it occupies and the interest on the loan that paid for it? What other resources do you currently lack and do you have a plan to acquire them? How essential are they to the future of your business? The costs of future acquisitions will need to be incorporated into your financial plan, and once you start thinking strategically, you should be examining the returns you are achieving on the capital invested in your inventory.

## Stockholding policies

These questions are primarily for retail and wholesale businesses, but also of interest to manufacturing firms holding stocks of raw materials and finished goods. What is the average value of the stock you are holding and in terms of days how does it compare with your sales revenue, i.e. is the stock being turned over at an acceptable rate, and how does this compare with the industry average? The average supermarket expects to turn over the tins of baked beans on its shelves every couple of days, and would be worried if that figure crept up to every two or three weeks. Do you have a realistic stock management policy? Are you always running short of stock, or are you holding too much? Have you established suitable reorder

31

level to accommodate your suppliers' delivery lead times? Are you rotating perishable stock? Do you have a control system that monitors receipts, issues and current quantities of each item? Can you monitor stock for theft or wastage? Do you have a system of stock valuation that links in with your financial accounts? Do you keep your records up to date? Stock control can be a major headache and a major loss of profit if it is not organized and maintained properly.

## Current and recurring problems within the business

Problems occur within business with annoying regularity, and are usually dealt with quickly and forgotten until they occur again. They may well be treated as isolated incidents, when in fact they may be indicative of recurrent or more serious underlying problems. Do you have any minor difficulties that seem to arise with annoying regularity? What are they really costing you, e.g. how much time do you or your staff spend on rectifying these in an average day, week or month? Would spending time to find a permanent solution be cheaper in the long run? How do the recurring problems affect staff morale? Do they affect your customers and their perception of your products or services? Are minor problems indicative of changes that need to be implemented in the business?

## Changes within the organization

Managing change is always a problem for any business, and more so if the change has resulted from a reactive decision rather than a proactive policy. What major changes have taken place in the business over the past year or two, and what changes are taking place at present? Were these changes planned in advance or were they the result of the need to respond to problems or new circumstances? Did they have any adverse effects on customers, staff or productivity levels? Were they implemented efficiently or could they have been done better?

Would you do things differently a second time around? What changes are you aware of that your business should seriously be considering? How urgent or threatening are these? What would be the costs, risks or negative effects of ignoring or deferring them, and can you really afford to take a chance with them?

The above points represent a fairly demanding and comprehensive series of questions about the performance of the business to date. By the time these have been examined, the owner-manager should have a critical and honest view of the business and its strengths and weaknesses which can be used as the basis for future actions and improvements. However, the real value of the process depends essentially on the owner-manager giving honest and realistic answers to the questions, and not hiding from questions or facts that might be uncomfortable to face up to.

## The market environment

**Who are our customers?**

This may seem like a ridiculous question but it is often surprising how little some businesses really know about their customers. For example, do they fit into stereotype groups (usually described as market segmentation), or do they share common characteristics in terms of their size and types of organization? How many customers of each type do you have, and which types generate the most profit for your business? What do you know about their buying patterns, e.g. the products they select, the volume of purchases and the frequency or regularity of orders? Have these patterns changed recently, and are the changes positive or negative? What are their key criteria for buying from you, as opposed to another supplier, e.g. low price, quality products or reliable service? Do you actually know who the decision-makers are in the businesses that buy from you, and when did you or one of your staff last speak with them?

## Customer base and customer loyalty

Are you able to retain customers or do they tend to change frequently? Of your total customers, how many of them trade with you on a regular basis? How many of them have been trading with you for more than twelve months? How do these various patterns compare with those of your competitors or other firms in the same industry? Are your customers loyal out of choice or because there is little competition? Do you think that they would be likely to recommend your good or services to others? How do you think your customers perceive you and your business – with respect, admiration, as reliable and honest, as someone they enjoy doing business with, or as a temporary stopgap, perhaps a cheapskate or necessary evil, or simply just convenient? The key to long-term retention of customers lies in ensuring that you are aware of their perceptions and expectations, and particularly of changes in these. Unless you are aware of changing perceptions and expectations, you cannot respond to them by modifying your products or services and the way they are provided, to keep the customers satisfied.

## Market share and recent trends

The answers to the questions in this section will depend very much on the size and nature of the market in which the business operates, e.g. whether it is local, national or international. Some markets are easy to break into, whilst others may have substantial barriers in terms of capital investment, heavy competition or the market being largely controlled by a few major players. The first task, then, is to define the market in which you see yourself operating; for example, you may be a major operator in the local market but small in relation to national operators. A good example of this is the UK real ale brewing industry, where there are multitude or quite new local micro breweries, about sixty established regional brewers (Wadworths, Shepherd Neame, Sam Smiths, Banks, Theakstons, etc.)

and a just handful of major national conglomerates which have resulted from a progressive series of mergers and takeovers (e.g. Scottish and Newcastle, Whitbread). The key question is then: just what market am I operating in? What is the total size, by volume of output or financial value, of that market? What proportion of that market do I control and has this increased or decreased recently? How easy is it to increase market share? What proportion of the market could I potentially control, and would the cost and effort of achieving the extra market share justify the increased profits?

## Quality standards and policies

Quality management is meant to be a continuous and ongoing process, but with the numerous demands and pressures which face owner-managers of small firms it is hardly surprising that those standards are often allowed to slip, and once this has happened it is much harder to re-establish them. So, do you currently have established written quality standards or policies? Can you remember what they are or when they were last reviewed? Are your employees aware of them? Are your customers aware of them? How do you promote the benefits of quality to your staff? How do you monitor and ensure the consistent achievement of quality standards within the business? What proportion of your outputs result in complaints or goods returned? How much time do you or your staff waste chasing problems that should not have occurred in the first place? What systems do you use to get feedback from your customers about the quality of your products or services? Is that feedback generally positive or negative? Finally, when you get negative feedback, how rapidly do you respond, and what do you do to rectify it?

## Current methods of advertising and promotion

Unless you are a marketing expert, advertising and promotion can be an expensive and time-consuming business. Once you find an advertising medium that works reasonably well, it is all too easy too continue using it without subsequent review or revision, until it sometimes becomes outdated and ineffective without you having realized the fact. Sales and promotion activities need continuous revision and monitoring to keep you ahead (or at least alongside) the competition. It is particularly important to monitor your advertising expenditure against the results it generates. So, what are your main methods of promoting and selling your goods or services? Are you happy with these, or do you just regard advertising as a necessary expense which must not be allowed to encroach too much on your profits? Have you changed your advertising recently? How often do you review its effectiveness? What methods to you use to monitor the returns on your advertising, e.g. by measuring levels of response to advertisements against the costs of these, the numbers of telephone enquiries converted into sales, or your sales staff's call rates and sales figures? How do your competitors promote their products? Do you compete head-on with these, or do you use different methods to sell your goods? What proportion of your sales revenue to you spend on sales and promotion, and do you think that this is adequate for current needs? Do you think you could increase your sales if you could afford more advertising? If so, why haven't you tried it?

## Competitors and their activity

Some industries or commercial activities are intensely competitive, particularly in areas such as research and development. Others, whilst still competitive, still co-operate to a certain extent with their rivals, often as a matter of efficiency. For example, licensed trade wholesalers compete heavily for customers, but still frequently work with each other to cover short-term stock shortages of particular products knowing that the favour will be reciprocated at a later date. They also often exchange information about bad and slow payers who may try to exploit the competitive nature of the market by playing them off against each other. In this situation, it makes sound business sense to treat competitors as an additional resource for the business, as it is often better to co-operate with a rival than for both parties to lose business. So, who are your competitors and where are they located? Do they pose a threat to your business, or can you all co-exist within the overall market? Do you have contact with them, or share information about difficult customers? Contact with competitors can also increase your market knowledge – to put it in a military context: if you can see the enemy then at least you know what he is doing; when you cannot see him, then is the time to worry!

## Competitive advantage

This concept is concerned with identifying the competitive advantages one business has over another and how these can be sustained. Lasher (1999, p. 51) claims that 'few firms have been able to achieve sustainable competitive advantage', i.e. to stay at the head of their market for a long period of time. So what? There may be a great deal of prestige in being the market leader, particularly in major international markets, but the average small business is not in that league, and its primary concern is that of achieving profitability rather than market share. However, the concept should not be passed by without first asking a few basic questions. First and foremost: what is it about my products and services that makes them stand out from the competition? What unique features do they have that makes people want to buy them as opposed to the alternatives? How can I ensure that this uniqueness persists? If that is not possible, what else can I do to keep ahead of my rivals? What can I do that will make my customers remember me and come back for more? The answers to these questions will start to form the options for the strategic marketing plan.

There are six main factors which normally apply for the analysis of the external environment: political, economic, social, technological, legislative and environmental, and these are often referred to as a PESTLE analysis after their initial letters. Inevitably, there is always some overlap between them because, for example, political decisions are often based on economic factors and are implemented via the legislative process. The fact remains that the PESTLE analysis is a useful tool to examine the external environment affecting large and small organizations alike.

**The external environment**

### Political issues

These tend to be issues which are generated at government (or increasingly at European Union) level, and which may have a direct impact on the day-to-day operation of the business. Some typical, recent examples might be the Statutory Minimum Wage, which guarantees a minimum hourly rate of pay for employees, or the Working Hours Directive. This was a politically motivated move which was imposed in the UK in 1998 on the grounds of 'health and safety' to ensure that British workers could not work more than specified hours, and thus render their employers more competitive than their continental rivals! The end result is that a major administrative burden has been placed on businesses which now have to monitor the working hours and overtime of all staff on a rolling basis to ensure compliance with the Directive. Naturally, this places a disproportionate burden on smaller firms that are less likely to have the administrative capacity. Similarly, the political move towards a single European currency will involve many small firms that will find themselves having to invoice their customers in Euros or risk losing the business to competitors. This is yet another example of political objectives which add to the financial and administrative burdens of small firms. Another current political issue is whether or not country sports such as fox hunting should be banned. The contentious proposal to ban blood sports is popular with many town-dwellers, but is seen as a threat to employment and small businesses (kennels, stables, blacksmiths, saddlers, etc.) in rural communities, where jobs are harder to find. Which political issues can you identify that have recently affected your business, or may do so in the future? Were these favourable or unfavourable to your business? What long-term effects are they likely to have?

### Economic factors

Economic cycles of high growth and prosperity changing to recession, and vice versa, are largely influenced by factors which are determined at national or international levels, for example exchange rates between international currencies, the key financial markets in London, Tokyo and New York. The government fiscal policies on inflation use interest rates as the primary control mechanism, but high interest rates push up currency values, which make imports cheaper and exports dearer, pushing down profit margins. Again, it is the smaller businesses with less resources which are most susceptible to the economic forces beyond their control. How often do you take notice or show interest in economic forecasts? What recent or current issues have affected your business and how did you respond to these? What issues are you aware of that may affect you in the future and how have you prepared for them?

### Social factors

Over the past thirty or forty years there have been major social and demographic changes in the population, including a higher proportion of the population who are living longer in retirement, a larger proportion of younger people who stay in education to a later age, and a social structure that has seen the demise of the old social classes and a major increase in ethnic groups. Most social changes occur relatively slowly and their impact on businesses is not always obvious at first, and a good example of this is the issue of Sunday trading. Thirty years ago, only a few newsagents, corner shops and off-licences opened on Sundays and then for very limited hours, and the Lord's Day Observance Society was most vociferous that this should stay the case. Today, only a very small percentage of the population actively follows the Christian faith, and for those who follow other beliefs, Sunday trading is quite natural, and for people with fast or busy lifestyles it is highly convenient. What social or demographic factors influence your business or affect the range of goods or services you offer to your customers? Are you making full use of the opportunities available to you? Do you actively target potential customers from other ethnic groups or are you missing out on a possible new market. Are you aware of any social factors that could influence your business in the near future, and what effects would these have on it? Are you ready for them?

## Technological factors

The fastest changes of all are occurring in technology and no small firm can afford to ignore it or live without it. In 1983, a 1 Mb computer with a basic accounting package would cost well over £5000, but now a highly sophisticated system with a full range of accounting and office software costs barely 10 per cent of that figure. As we discussed in Chapter 1, changes in technology have not created a leisure age but have instead created the need for people constantly to upgrade their skills to remain employable. Similarly, if businesses do not constantly embrace and engage in new technologies they risk being left behind by rivals who do so. Is your business making full use of current technology at the present time? If not, what plans do you have to improve its use? What applications do you currently operate? Could your systems be developed to provide better (more accurate or useful) financial information, or to provide better communications with you customers? Are you and your staff adequately skilled to make the best use of technology? If not, what do you have to do to rectify the situation?

## Legislation – current and future

The range of legislation affecting businesses is constantly changing and increasing, now coming from both the British government and the European Union. In the eyes of the law ignorance is no defence, so it is the responsibility of the owner-manager to keep abreast of changing legislation and the implications for the business. This applies both to general legislation affecting all organizations such as health and safety regulations, pollution control, disability discrimination and employment law, and to industry-specific regulations such as controls over abattoirs, and food storage, processing and handling that have affected the food industry in recent years. Are you aware of the changes in legislation which have taken place over the past two or three years? How do these affect your business? Are you sure that you are already fully compliant with these and the possible consequences of non-compliance? Are there any new regulations in the pipeline with which you must comply in the future? What will be the cost implications of complying with these?

## Environmental issues and controls

Since the Control of Pollution Act (1974), there has been a steady stream of environmental legislation to complement the increasing public awareness of environmental issues, and this will not go away. Most of it does benefit the environment, but inevitably this has a financial impact on businesses both large and small. One of the most recent positive examples is the regulation requiring that a specific minimum proportion of all packaging should be recycled. A less enthralling example is the current political objective to reduce pollution by imposing high taxes on road fuel; this may seem environmentally friendly (or is it really just an excuse to raise indirect taxation?) but as fuel prices increase motorists naturally look for the lowest prices. These lower prices are typically found in service stations run by the multinational oil companies and the major supermarket chains, against whom small local independent garages cannot compete. As stated above, environmental issues and regulations will not go away, so the businesses that will best be able to handle them will be those which take a proactive stance and prepare to work with them. What environmental changes or issues are you aware of that might affect your business? What impact are they likely to have on your operations and your profitability? What preparations have you made to accommodate these?

Invariably, any strategic analysis of a business, particularly where lending banks are concerned, must contain a SWOT analysis – where the strengths and weaknesses of the business are listed (i.e. the internal factors – staff and management skills, gaps which need filling, etc.), and the opportunities and threats (the external factors) are identified, and frequently underestimated. The SWOT analysis can be a very valuable and useful tool, but it must be used in a positive and productive manner. The strengths and weaknesses should really reflect the answers to the questions that have been posed in the analysis of the internal environment, and similarly the opportunities and threats will relate to issues which have been identified in the analyses of the market and external environments.

*The SWOT analysis*

Frequently, the SWOT is treated superficially and is insufficiently checked or validated, therein wasting a useful opportunity – simply going through the motions of preparing a SWOT may keep the bank manager happy but it does not really do justice to the potential future of the business. Ideally, the person carrying out the analysis should ask another person (preferably one with an objective insight into the business) to carry out an independent analysis so that the results of the two can be compared, evaluated and if necessary mediated. This is particularly important when the SWOT analysis is being carried out to assess the skills of the owner-managers and key staff. It is all too easy to overestimate management capabilities, and to underestimate weaknesses. If there should be any major gaps or areas of deficiency, these would almost certainly affect the successful implementation of the business strategy. So, when did you last carry out a SWOT analysis on yourself and your business, and isn't it about time you made a start?

## *References*

Johnson, G. and Scholes, K. (1997). *Exploring Corporate Strategy*, 4th Edn. Prentice Hall.

Lasher, W. (1999). *Strategic Thinking for Smaller Businesses and Divisions*. Blackwell.

Mintzberg, H. (1994). *The Rise and Fall of Strategic Planning*. New York: Free Press.

## *Further reading*

Bennett, R. (1996). *Corporate Strategy and Business Planning*. Pitman.

Bennett, R. (1998). *Small Business Survival*. NatWest/Financial Times.

Bowman, C. and Asch, D. (1996). *Managing Strategy*. Macmillan.

# Chapter 3 Planning for the future – where are we going?

Chapter 3
Chapter 3

This chapter is concerned with the fundamental decisions about where the business is moving and how it will develop in the future. It forms the context and key objectives for the subsequent chapters that will focus on the specific policies and strategies (marketing, finance, personnel, etc.) which will facilitate the achievement of those objectives. In terms of the Revised Business Development Standards, it relates to Unit A2: Develop your plans for the business, and Unit D2: Take key decisions that will affect the business.

## Mission statements

Over the past ten or fifteen years, much has been made of the need for every organization to have a Vision or Mission Statement which specifies (frequently in a grandiose fashion) the key objectives of the organization. The mission statement is heralded for all to see as a proud emblem of the organization's customer focus and an inspiration for the employees. Lasher (1999, p. 31) summarizes this quite well: 'The vision (of a company) is reflected in a mission statement which summarizes the overall goals and values of the organization as succinctly as possible. The purpose of the mission statement is to communicate these ideas to interested parties, especially the employees'. Cole (1994, p. 18) defines it as 'a public statement on behalf of an organization which sets out its raison d'etre in terms of the customer needs it intends to satisfy, the markets in which it will meet those needs, and the manner in which it will meet them'.

In many organizations, the mission statement does have a useful and positive function. This is typically in those organizations which regard it as a working tool against which achievement is measured, and which is itself periodically reviewed, and where both the objectives and the measurement of achievement are communicated to the employees. In others it is a 'must-have' (because all other important and successful businesses have one, don't they?) that bears little relevance to the ongoing operation and long-term development of the business. To state the obvious, there is little point in having a mission statement if you do not intend to implement it.

The point to be drawn from this is that if you intend to summarize or formulate your primary objectives in such a format, then there must be some practical and measurable purpose behind it, and it must be realistic and achievable. For example, a local butcher might dream to aspire to become 'The largest and most profitable butchery business in the UK' and perhaps in twenty or thirty years this might be achieved, but the strategic plan for the business cannot practically look twenty years ahead. The key to successful growth and development of small firms lies in their ability to respond flexibly and rapidly to market change and customer needs. Therefore, the strategic plan for the small business can only realistically focus on what can be forecast as likely to happen over the next two or three years, or five years at the most, as distinct from large conglomerates which can plan their strategies over five to ten years because they are sufficiently large to be able to exert some influence over the market in which they operate. In the smaller market, the chances are that within three years local circumstances will change, and when the changes occur, the policies and ambitions of the owner-manager will have to change to meet them. Back to our butcher then, a more realistic mission statement might be 'to become the first choice supplier of high quality fresh meat and produce in the district', which would be a perfectly realistic and achievable objective within two or three years. In the longer term, the strategic objective might be extended with the opening of other shops 'to become the first choice local butchery service throughout the county'. Alternatively, as pressure from the large out-of-town supermarkets increases, the objective might be modified so as 'to maintain a profitable chain of independent high street butchery shops represented in each major town in the county'. This recognizes the changes in purchasing patterns of the general public where the convenience of shopping in one location often outweighs quality produce and individual service. More to the point, it illustrates that mission statements are not written in stone and will change over the years in response to external and market influences.

**What do you personally want to achieve?**

This is the first question the owner-manager must consider, as his or her personal ambitions are integral to the direction the business will take. A person with great personal ambitions for wealth and prosperity will want the same for the business as the business will hopefully become the vehicle that delivers that wealth. Another person who is just running the business as a hobby, perhaps earning some extra cash by doing something they enjoy, will have far lower personal and business expectations.

The ambitions which individuals hold for themselves are often determined by their own personal parameters – their financial circumstances and family responsibilities, their background and previous experiences, etc. – and here we are touching on the realms of psychology and Maslow's Hierarchy or needs. The entrepreneur with a dependant family will want to create sufficient income and wealth to provide them with a comfortable and safe environment. However, the extent of their ambition over and above that may well depend on other motivations and possibly behavioural factors. For example, the extent of their own competitive nature, whether or not they have experienced former wealth or deprivation, whether their ambition and drive is linked to the need for prestige and esteem. In the example of the hobby-business mentioned above, for a person with adequate income (perhaps from a spouse or partner) the primary motivation is personal satisfaction rather than the generation of income. So what are your personal ambitions, financial needs and motivations? Are you in business purely to make money? Are you looking for job satisfaction? Is status and recognition important to you? Do you feel that you have a responsibility for the employment of your staff? Or are you motivated by a combination of these? How will these personal ambitions affect the way you operate your business? The answers to these questions will largely determine what you personally want to achieve, which will in turn decide whether the business stays as it is, changes direction, or proceeds to develop and grow.

## What long-term objectives do you have for the business?

So, now you have considered the personal issues and questions in the previous section, you will be able to synthesize from your personal objectives some form of overall direction for the business that can subsequently be translated into a key objective or mission statement for the business itself. Using the earlier example: 'I want to develop and expand my butchery business to provide a good level of income for myself and my family, and a long-term investment and legacy for my children', becomes: 'I want the butchery business to survive and prosper in the long-term and to generate good profits on a regular basis'. In turn, translating this into a more customer-focused mission statement, this becomes 'Our objective is to maintain a profitable chain of independent high street butchery shops, supplying quality produce, in each major town in the county'.

It is quite interesting that an analysis of the growth aspirations of smaller firms, conducted by the Cambridge Small Business Research Centre (Storey, 1994, p. 120), revealed that of the sample population interviewed approximately 64.3 per cent of small and 65.7 per cent of micro firms were interested in moderate as opposed to substantial growth, and 10.4 per cent of small firms and 13.2 per cent of micro firms wanted to stay the same size; 1.7 and 2.7 per cent respectively wanted to grow smaller, whilst a quite modest 22.9 and 17.0 per cent respectively were looking for substantial growth. Growth, particularly for its own sake, is by no means the most significant focal point or objective for owner-managers.

This question raises the key issues of defining the strategic options for the business. Johnson and Scholes (1997) argue that strategic options need to be examined in terms of Generic Strategies, Directions and Methods:

*What options are available to achieve the objectives?*

- Their generic strategies consist of three alternatives. First, Cost Leadership, which is the strategy by which businesses maintain competitive advantage in the marketplace by planning and managing the cost structure (comparative price) of their goods and services in relation to that of their competitors. Second is the Differentiation strategy, which focuses on product choice, quality, service and perceived value in the eyes of the customer. For small firms, this is often more feasible than the cost leadership option, where as new entrants to the market, they may not be able to achieve the same economies of scale available to established competitors. Third is the Focus strategy, whereby the organization targets its efforts towards one or more specific niches in the market; this, in particular, is a frequently used means by which small firms can achieve market share in the face of competition from bigger rivals. The drawback, however, is that too much success by a small firm in a niche market can attract unwelcome attention from powerful and more wealthy competitors. There is an additional hybrid strategy proposed by Lasher (1999, p. 87), that of Best-cost Provider, which combines cost leadership with differentiation, e.g. providing a high-quality product at a mid-range price.

- The directions in which organizations can move are quite varied. The most obvious is the 'do nothing' option which, whilst it may be unthinkable in most larger businesses, is often perfectly acceptable to the small firm owner-manager, particularly if the current situation accommodates their own personal needs and aspirations. Johnson and Scholes cite the 'Withdrawal' option as being one that is often overlooked. In some cases, it is the owner-manager's specific intent to develop the business to a certain size and then to sell it as a going concern. In other cases, if the future prospects are looking grim then a strategic withdrawal from all or part of the market may be the soundest decision to make. A stage of 'consolidation' may be chosen wherein the firm makes no move to expand or grow, but prefers to focus on its internal operations to improve its efficiency and profitability. More positive options include moves to increase 'market penetration' to sell greater volumes of current products or services in the existing market, 'market development' to sell existing products in new segments of the market, or alternatively 'product development' to expand by developing new products for the market. Another option is to diversify the product range. 'Related diversification' is the process of expanding the product range beyond the current situation but remaining within the same industry, e.g. where our butcher friend from the earlier example decides to start making and selling meat pies. 'Unrelated diversification' occurs when the business moves into a different line of products or services, e.g. when our butcher decides to expand his shop to sell fish, or fruit and vegetables. The latter would be an example of horizontal integration where the butcher is selling complementary products, but the diversification process could also involve backward integration, e.g. where the butcher acquired a livestock farm or an abattoir, or such as the Shepherd Neame brewery in Kent, which owned its own hop farm. The integration could also move forwards, for example if a small independent brewery decided to acquire one or two pubs through which its products could be sold, or if a market garden opened a farm shop to sell the produce it was growing direct to the public.

● Johnson and Scholes identified three main methods by which organizations could develop. The first of these is 'internal development', i.e. growing from within, using its own or borrowed resources to expand or to develop new products, particularly if it does not have sufficient resources, e.g. to buy another business to facilitate rapid growth. Second, by 'acquisition', wherein the business buys or takes over another business either in its own market to increase market share or economies of scale, or as part of the diversification process to gain a broader product base. This is often the easiest and fastest method of expansion or diversification when resources are not limited, or when the barriers to entry into a new market are substantial. Third, by means of 'joint development', where, for example, two or more businesses co-operate in the development of a new product or venture. This consortium approach is more likely to occur between large organizations involved in major projects (e.g. civil engineering or aircraft design), but in the small firms situation the joint development may take the form of the franchising of products or services to achieve growth.

Moving back to the original question (where do you want your business to go?), the key questions to be asked are:

● Do I want to keep the business or to sell or liquidate it?

● If I keep it, do I stay as I am or do I wish to change or grow the business?

● If I do not change, do I continue to trade as at present, or do I consolidate, i.e. focus on improving efficiency and profitability?

● If I decide to develop the business, do I want to (a) grow it by being more competitive, (b) grow it by developing, or diversifying into, a wider range of products or services, or (c) grow it by focusing on niche markets?

● If I opt to increase market penetration, do I achieve this by increasing my own sales and marketing activities, or

**Case Study 1: Folke-stone whelks**

For many years, Folkestone Harbour has reputedly sold the best whelks in England, with an almost perfectly competitive market situation operating between the vendors. Five small seafood stalls and a wet-fish shop sell their whelks of similar quality, at broadly similar prices, with similar trimmings, in similar containers. Two or three open every day, but several open just at week-ends or daily in mid-summer. They compete with each other but co-exist, and have done so for scores of years, visited by generations of day-trippers from London, with their children and grandchildren.

However, traditional tastes are changing and in recent years day-trippers have wanted more than just a bowl of whelks, winkles, shrimps, cockles, mussels or jellied eels, all liberally doused with chilli vinegar. But behind the seafood stall lies an interesting pattern of generic strategies. Although none have opted for a cost leader-ship approach, two have achieved backward integration with boats moored nearby to catch their own produce. One of those has also integrated forwards as a whole-saler supplying other stalls and wet-fish shops in nearby towns. One has opted for market penetration by acqui-sition, now owning two of the outlets. One has chosen market development by diversifying, i.e. by purchasing wet fish from other trawlers and selling it to the general public. The final stallholder has chosen product devel-opment by offering hot and spicy cooked seafood, dressed salads and escargots alongside the conventional fare (well, he is French), and horizontal diversification with an adjacent stall selling burgers and hot dogs to the day-trippers' kids.

They continue to co-exist side-by-side, the day-trippers still flock to the harbour at weekends and summer holi-days come sun, rain, wind or hail, and the whelks are reckoned to be as good as ever – if you like whelks that is!

do I seek to acquire another business and its share of the market?

- If I decide to develop my market share by offering a wider range of products or services, do I develop this within the business using my own or borrowed capital? Do I develop these in co-operation with another business, perhaps in a foreign market that is not in direct competition with my own? Or do I buy them in from another supplier, perhaps under licence or in a franchise arrangement?

- Is there any advantage to be gained by integration, backwards forwards or horizontal, e.g. by developing subsidiary parts of the business or buying a related business? Will the cost savings or extra profit from this be comparable with what could be generated by an alternative strategy, e.g. by market development or penetration?

## Which option is best for my business?

Finding the answer to this question requires a systematic evaluation of the strategic options, i.e. the process of answering the questions raised in the previous section, but in the context of the strategic analysis of the organization. Again, Johnson and Scholes (1997) have come up with a suitable method based on three main factors:

- Suitability: to what extent the strategic options are compatible with the strategic analysis of the organization, its operating environment, and its strengths and weaknesses. Would a particular option make full use of the organization's strengths whilst at the same time avoiding any adverse impact by its weaknesses or any foreseeable external factors such as changes in legislation or government policy?

- Feasibility: this examines how and whether or not the strategy might work in practice. For example, an option to expand into export markets might not be feasible if the business had no knowledge or experience of exporting and lacked the economies of scale to compete on price against the local suppliers in those markets. Similarly, the option to grow market share by acquiring another business would be totally unrealistic if the business had little or no spare capital and borrowing capacity to finance the acquisition. In the case of the small firm, the feasibility of any option in terms of the firm's capacity and resources will always be the limiting factor.

- Acceptability: how acceptable and compatible it will be relative to the needs and objectives of the stakeholders in the business. An option that appeals to one stakeholder may be totally unacceptable to another. This is a situation that can frequently arise in partnerships and small family firms, when one partner wants to grow and expand whilst another wants to avoid risk and just consolidate the business. A similar situation might be where one director wants to focus on market penetration for current products or services, and another wants to diversify the business. In an ideal world, the business might be able to follow both strategies, but in small firms the financial resources rarely permit such luxuries.

In terms of practical decision-making methods that can be used to evaluate alternative options, there are a wide range of models, tools and techniques available. These range from the ever-popular SWOT, through a range of financial methods such as cost-benefit analysis, payback periods, liquidity and financial ratios, return-on-capital-employed calculations, net present value, cash-flow and profit forecasts, to more complicated models, which are designed to forecast market share, analyse the sensitivity of the market and evaluate stakeholder support. It is not intended to describe these individually here, as they could fill a book in their own right, and they are more than adequately described in books dedicated to the subject, e.g. Gore et al. (1992). The choice of appropriate methods will be largely determined by the nature of the primary objectives themselves. For example, a business objective relating to long-term profit generation will most likely use financial techniques to evaluate available options: profit forecasts, return on capital employed, etc. An objective based on expansion and market share, however, might use statistical models or techniques to compare potential growth rates, sensitivity or an analysis of market trends and opportunities.

The biggest problem for an owner-manager is to identify the right method for their particular needs, and this is where specialist advice may be well worth paying for. Potential sources of advice and guidance might include chartered accountants or management consultants (both relatively expensive), bank managers (with a possible tendency to focus on your borrowing capacity or matching it to what they have to offer), marketing consultants, local enterprise agency business advisors and local business links. The latter two may be the most appropriate for smaller businesses because they are more impartial, and tend to cost less, often offering a free initial consultation and fixed fee advice. The government is currently in the process of introducing its Small Business Service, which will co-ordinate the activities of the various support agencies to better support small firms. Whatever source of advice you choose, any objective factual analysis of the pros and cons of the various options should also take due account of your own personal objectives as owner-manager of the business, because you have to be comfortable with the final choice to make it work. Remember that the strategy of the business should aim to match its internal strengths and resources to the needs of the marketplace, whilst remaining within the parameters defined by its stakeholders.

So, in order to evaluate the various options that have been identified, we must ask a further range of questions:

- Which of the selected options are most compatible with the strengths and weaknesses that were identified in the strategic analysis of the business? Do they build on the strengths? Do they avoid or overcome the weaknesses?

- How do the options relate to the opportunities and threats that have been identified, and do they take full advantage of those opportunities? Are they robust enough to withstand any obvious threats?

- What external factors (changes in government policy, legislation, economic trends, etc.) could influence the various options, and would the effects of these factors be positive or negative?

- Are the options compatible with the objectives of the owners of the business, and if this is not the case, are the differences minor, substantial or critical?

- Are there any factors within the options which might be regarded as unacceptable by other stakeholders, such as suppliers, financiers or bankers?

- What risks are associated with each of the options, and are these regarded as acceptable by the owners and stakeholders involved in the business?

- Is the business capable of accommodating or implementing any changes implicit in the various options?

- What are the current limiting factors that might inhibit the options? For example, financial resources, borrowing capacity, physical space, management skills, staff availability and skills, market size and accessibility. How might these limiting factors be overcome?

- Given current resources, which of the proposed options could realistically be achieved by the business in the next three to five years?

- What returns (in terms of increased revenue, cost savings, improved profits, etc.) might we expect from the respective options, and what levels of investment would be required to achieve those returns?

The mission statement and primary objectives of the business are insufficient in their own right to provide a practical basis for growth and development. The broad strategic or primary objectives of the organization need to be broken down into a series of subsidiary objectives relating to specific functional areas, operational areas or management units within the business. These specific objectives should be compatible with each other and should complement the primary objective. Lasher (1999) describes this as the process of upward support, essential to ensure the co-ordination of the subsidiary objectives to avoid management and strategic problems, conflicts between operational areas of the organization, etc.

*Defining the business objectives to meet the chosen option*

For example, a primary objective 'to grow the business by 20 per cent per annum over each of the next five years' does not mean that each functional area of the business must grow by no less (or no more) than 20 per cent per annum. The specific objectives for each department may be totally different for practical reasons. The sales department may have a target to increase output by 30 per cent in year one, although the cost of doing so may only raise sales revenue by 15 per cent in the first instance. The production department may need to double its capacity in year one, and again in year four to meet the overall target, as this may be less disruptive, and more practical and cost-effective than increasing output by 20 per cent each year. For the finance department, the target may be to implement a new invoicing and customer accounts system within six months, and for marketing there may be a need to design a new image for the company's products within the next three months. Personnel may need to recruit and train new staff in readiness for the expanded production capacity and staff in the retail customers' outlets will need product training. Some of these objectives are longer term (i.e. strategic in their own right), whilst others are tactical and relate to the shorter-term implementation of the strategy.

For objectives to work effectively they need to meet a number of criteria:

- They need to be challenging, i.e. achievable but stretching performance beyond what is currently achieved, or what could be easily achieved. However, the resulting increase in performance may need to be rewarded in some way if the motivation of staff is to be maintained, and if further increases in performance are subsequently sought.

- They must be SMART. Specific, so as to define targets in a manner that can be clearly understood. Measurable, to enable their achievement (or otherwise) to be accurately assessed. Achievable in terms of the capabilities of the staff or business units assigned to meet them. Realistic in terms of the resources made available to achieve them. Timely in terms of the target period or deadline within which they must be achieved.

- Within the objectives, we must build in key success factors, i.e. performance indicators that indicate that the key stages of the objectives are being achieved.

- At a less strategic level, Cole (1994, p. 17) states that explicit goals and objectives provide standards of performance which can be used to motivate staff, and (p. 29) objectives are 'the short-term and specific intentions of the various operational units of the organization. They are often called targets and are key elements in the tactical plans' of the organization. Personally, I regard the word 'target' as more appropriate to the short-term operational plans concerned with day-to-day output and efficiency.

- Objectives should complement each other, and should not conflict with each other.

- The objectives should be explicit so that they can be easily understood. They should be 'sold' to staff to ensure that the staff take ownership of them to improve the prospects of their achievement. If the employees do not understand or relate to the objectives, or the importance of them to the organization, then there is no guarantee that they will co-operate with their implementation. Indeed, if they are not sold on the importance of the objectives to the organization, they may well positively interfere with their implementation.

Questions to be asked when formulating the functional objectives that support the chosen policy for development of the business are as follows:

- Are the defined objectives compatible with and supportive of the primary objective of business development?

- Are the objectives of the various functional areas compatible with each other, or do they contain conflicting elements?

- Do the objectives meet the SMART criteria?

- Will they stretch the functional departments of the organization and their staff?

- Do the staff understand the objectives, and do they accept their relevance and importance to the future of the organization?

*References*

Cole, G. A. (1994). *Strategic Management*. DP Publications.

Gore, C., Murray, K. and Richardson, W. (1992). *Strategic Decision Making*. Cassell.

Johnson, G. and Scholes, K. (1997). *Exploring Corporate Strategy*, 4th Edn. Prentice Hall.

Lasher, W. (1999). *Strategic Thinking for Smaller Businesses and Divisions*. Blackwell.

Storey, D. (1994). *Understanding the Small Business Sector*. Thomson Business Press.

*Further reading*

Bennett, R. (1996). *Corporate Strategy and Planning*. Pitman.
Gore, C., Murray, K. and Richardson, W. (1992). *Strategic Decision Making*. Cassell.
Porter, M. E. (1985). *Competitive Advantage: Creating and Sustaining A Superior Performance*. Free Press.

# Chapter 4 What resources
# Chapter 4 will we need?
## Chapter 4

Once the strategic choices have been made, and the objectives have been determined and agreed, the next phase involves the tactical decisions, that is the staged implementation of the strategies in the medium term. The first question that springs immediately to mind is 'What resources will we need to do it?' Broadly speaking, we are talking about premises, space, plant and equipment, transport, office equipment and computers, communications equipment, raw materials or stock, packaging, advertising materials, staff and managers to make productive use of it all, and of course the money to pay for everything. However, before the acquisitions can begin there are still a large number of crucial decisions that have to be made, as many of these purchases will involve substantial long-term capital investment, and few businesses (particularly smaller ones) can afford to make expensive mistakes.

The financial and personnel issues will be examined in later chapters. Chapter 4 is concerned with the S/NVQ Units E1 and E2, which concern making the best use of premises and equipment, and to Unit K1, which is about negotiating and contracting with suppliers. The chapter will examine a range of questions relating to these Units.

## Premises

There is no specific formula for finding the ideal location for business premises although, clearly, the nature of the market will have fundamental implications for the location and vice versa. With the exception of e-commerce and mail order firms, whose clients are distance-based, the business needs to reflect the community it serves, and therefore its location within that community must be selected to match the needs of that community. A business selling commercial hydraulic hoses and their fittings is ideally situated in an industrial estate, where its commercial clients can call and can park easily, but it would be as much out of place in the high street as a fine china shop would be in an industrial estate. Equally, the location of competitors must be considered. Where the market community is large, it is not unusual to see competing businesses located nearby each other, but in a smaller community, two rivals competing for the same small market would probably put each other out of business as neither would make enough profit to survive. It is also important that the location should match the image of the product or service on offer, and more so that the premises themselves should reflect that image. It is not sufficient that the fine china shop is situated in the high street, it must be at the right side or end of the high street where more affluent customers are likely to be found, and it must project an image of up-market quality. So then, a few questions to ponder:

- What space or premises do I currently have available, and will these be adequate for the future? Most new firms start their existence by selecting the premises that match their immediate needs at the lowest affordable cost, so as not to eat into valuable working capital. They can seldom afford space for future expansion and in consequence often find themselves faced with moving premises at least once in the first two or three years, which is an expensive and disruptive process. Faced then with the desire or necessity to expand, the obvious first step is to review the current premises. Very often, what looks like an overcrowded building is one in which space is simply being utilized badly, in particular vertical space. So, can a move be avoided by better use of existing space? Is there an opportunity to use storage racking, or perhaps to install

a mezzanine to free up floor space? Is there an opportunity to extend the building in any way? If the answer
is no, and a move is essential, then you must move on
to the next question.

• What space or premises will I require for the future? Well,
just how far into the future are you looking? If you have
completed a strategic analysis of your business and identified the direction(s) for your growth, along with some
realistic and quantified objectives, this should not be too
much of a problem. For a service business, for which the
moving process is usually less complicated than a manufacturing or distribution business, the size of premises
may be of less significance than their location in relation
to the market community. However, for a manufacturing
firm, the growth objectives may require substantial capital
investment in production machinery and storage space.

• How much extra space will I need? The chosen site will
need to be sufficiently large to accommodate the extra plant
and equipment for a number of years, and ideally having
sufficient surrounding area to accommodate further
expansion at a later date. With the high costs of relocation,
measured in terms of disruption to output as well as the
cost of physically moving, it is realistic to look for premises
that will be adequate for at least the next five years and ideally ten years, otherwise your surplus profits and reserves
will be swallowed up by repeated relocations. This may
mean that you are paying for space which is not being fully
utilized in the earlier stages, but you can always sub-let it
until you need it for your own use. It may be easier to lease
a site that is initially too large than to have to buy out the
leases of your immediate neighbours in order to expand a
year or two later. If you have sufficient capital, you may
look to buy a site with adequate space to add additional
buildings, as you need them. Remember, you are in business to make a profit for yourself and your shareholders,
not for the benefit of estate agents, solicitors, landlords and
mortgage lenders!

- How soon will I need to expand and what sort of lead time is involved? It is often the lead time that determines the how soon. If you are aware that your premises are becoming tight and will be inadequate within a year, then the time to look is now. It can often take months of searching to find the right place and to negotiate the right deal for its lease or purchase. The more time you have available, then the more chance you will have of negotiating terms to your own benefit. For example, it is quite common for a landlord who has been sitting on empty premises to agree to an initial rent-free period of three to six months, which can be a great help towards recovering the costs of relocation and refitting the new premises. It can also facilitate the ease of relocation by enabling you to prepare the new premises so that you can relocate with minimal disruption to your customers. In terms of lead times, it can sometimes take months to find the right site. Subsequent to finding the site, it is also quite common for solicitors to take a further three months to negotiate and complete the terms of a lease, especially if you require finance from a bank or commercial mortgage lender.

- Should I relocate to another area? The answer to this question will depend on several factors: the location of your customers, the location of your competitors, and any incentives that might influence your relocation. As discussed earlier, if your customers are very local, then there will be nothing to be gained by moving away from them, and you should be thinking in terms of locating your business at a site where you will be readily accessible to them. If your customers are remote, e.g. supplied by mail order or delivery service, then you stand to benefit by any cost savings gained through relocation. Certainly, you should not consider relocation if it puts you at a disadvantage in relation to your competitors, unless of course there are compelling financial gains to be made. Regional or Rural Development Agencies are often able to offer substantial financial incentives to move into designated development areas such as Scotland, Wales and Romney Marsh (funny how all of these places seem to be full of sheep!). The main objective of these incentives is to generate local employment opportunities, so you must first ask yourself if such a move would create problems in finding suitably skilled or qualified staff in that area. Think about it – will there be many precision engineers or software programmers to be found amongst the local shepherds?

- What sort of a contractual arrangement should I be thinking about? The three most common options are to rent, lease or buy. Renting usually requires relatively little outlay up front, typically three months' rent in advance. The duration of the rental agreement is usually negotiable, but if you hope to get an initial rent-free period, it is unlikely to be less than two years. If you think that there is a chance you will outgrow the premises, say after five years, you may sign up for such a period with the option to extend the rental period after that date. The landlord will invariably insist on regular rent reviews, and reviews always go upwards, so be sure to use an experienced solicitor or agent to negotiate on your behalf to avoid any commitments that might adversely affect your profits. Long-term leases on premises avoid the spiralling costs of rent reviews and provide a known fixed level of future overhead costs (ground rent, council business rates, etc.), but do require an initial capital outlay to buy the lease. On a long-term lease, the capital outlay can probably be recovered by selling the lease at a later date, often showing a profit. There is, however, the drawback under English law whereby if a subsequent purchaser of the lease should default on ground rent then the liability will usually revert to the previous leaseholder. In the past, this has left some businesses finding themselves liable for overhead costs on premises they no longer occupy, and which cannot be sold because of legal distraints, or charges against the site held by mortgage lenders. If you are in the fortunate position of having surplus capital, or the private resources to offer a second guarantee against a commercial mortgage, then it might pay to consider buying the freehold of suitable premises. This would offer the benefits of regular and foreseeable future outgoings coupled with the prospect of capital growth, although to gain the full benefits it would probably be necessary to stay on the site for at least five to ten years. Whatever option you choose, the key factor to remember is that you should never deplete or use your working capital to pay for fixed assets.

- How much will each type cost? There is no answer to this one. Relative costs will vary from month to month according to interest rates and local demand for commercial property. Costs of similar premises may vary widely between districts just a few miles apart depending on local availability, local services, accessibility to road networks, etc. A cost comparison of the various options is essential but cost should not be the only consideration, as it is no good having cheap premises if they are not accessible by your customers, or not located near your markets.

- What options are available to fund the expansion? There are always costs attached to moving premises, and if these cannot be financed from profits or reserves, then medium- or long-term bank loans (three to five years) may be the answer, although some form of security will invariably be required for these. Commercial mortgages are available to finance leases or to buy property, typically over ten- to fifteen-year periods, but the lender will require a deposit, typically 20–25 per cent of the full cost to be provided up front by the borrower. The precise figures will depend on the age and value of the premises, or the residual period of the lease etc., and legal fees and expenses will also be incurred in the process. Some of the options for acquiring and financing premises are examined in more detail in Butler (2000, Chapters 8 and 12).

- What do I have at present and is it adequate for my current needs? We have to start with a critical and objective assessment of the current inventory. How old is it, and how much useful life does it have? Is it paid for or is there still outstanding finance due? Is it currently reliable or are we losing money as a result of frequent downtime for repairs and maintenance, and if so what is the frequency and average cost of breakdowns? It may well be that the cost of repeated repairs and maintenance may be less per annum than the cost of leasing of buying new equipment. Are there alternatives available that offer higher rates of output or a better potential return on their cost? Do the manufacturers have anything new in the pipeline that could be worth a few months' wait? Are our competitors gaining a march on us by using better or more cost-effective machinery? Before you think that you have all of the answers to these questions, just check back with your staff who actually use the plant or equipment, and ask them for their honest opinions, as these may surprise you. They will often be able to identify problems (or potential solutions) of which you are not aware.

- Is it likely to be adequate for my future needs, or do I need more production capacity? Those future needs will have been largely determined by the strategic choices you have made. If you are planning to adopt a policy of expansion by market penetration, and still have spare production capacity available, then further capital outlay may not be necessary. However, if you plan to expand by diversifying your product range then current equipment may be of little use beyond that of maintaining output of current product lines. This is where the need for accurate sales and marketing forecasts become critical, as you must decide on the right amount of capital investment to match your long-term production plans. If you invest too little, there is the risk or running out of production capacity far too soon, and facing further investment before adequate profits are available to pay for it. If your forecasts are too high, you risk having expensive plant and production capacity laying idle and burdening you with disproportionate overhead costs. The ideal compromise is to plan your growth in progressive stages which can be financed out of ongoing profits; however, where high-tech manufacturing equipment is concerned this is not always practical, as to buy several smaller installations of plant may prove far more expensive than a single large installation.

- Can I afford not to invest in new plant or equipment? There always remains the 'do nothing' option, but sooner or later, current equipment will wear out. Even if the owner-manager has no ambitions for expansion there is always a need to keep pace with changes in customer demand over a period of time, and even traditional craft industries have to modify their practice and methods occasionally to keep themselves competitive and their products affordable. Perhaps the question should be supplemented with another: how long can I expect to stay in business if I don't invest in the business at some stage? It was systematic lack of investment in new steel and shipbuilding technology that contributed to the decline of these industries in Britain in the latter half of the twentieth century.

- Should I be investing in new technology? The answer will depend on what possible advantages the use of technology can provide over your competitors. New technology can make a great contribution towards competitive strategy; for example, if it gives you a cost advantage such as a cost saving, compared with what your competitors can achieve, then this may assist with your cost leadership strategy. The advantages could lie elsewhere in terms of increased quality or more flexibility in product design, enabling some diversification of your product range. There really has to be some tangible and measurable advantage to be gained from employing new technology, rather than just using it for its own sake, and in some markets in which customers value traditional craftsmanship, technology can be a disadvantage. They key issue then is whether or not the use of technology will complement and help the firm to achieve its strategic objectives.

● How do I assess the best option? This is where you must decide on a policy against which you can evaluate the relative costs. Are you going to look for the quickest payback, i.e. the fastest recovery of capital invested, or will you seek the highest percentage return on the money invested, which may take longer but could offer a higher total profit? When you are examining these options, remember to include all of the costs involved and not just the basic cost of the new plant or equipment. You must include the costs of financing the purchase, not just in terms of interest paid, but the investment income you may have lost by using your reserves. You must also try to calculate and include all of the other costs that relate to the purchase and installation of new equipment, including lost production caused by disruption, physical installation costs, staff training and the commissioning period until full output is achieved once again. Finally, what, if any, is the cost of disruption, in terms of lost business?

● Do I need to operate my own vehicles? The first question: why do you operate them now? If your customers are local, i.e. situated within a reasonable driving distance, and need regular and reliable deliveries, then it is probably more cost-effective to operate your own vehicles. For example, wholesalers who supply local retail outlets (shops, restaurants, pubs, leisure facilities) on a regular and frequent basis will usually choose to deliver direct, and indeed the contact with customers during deliveries can be a valuable part of the sales process. Less frequent direct deliveries may also be viable given sufficient value

*Transport and distribution*

or volume of goods being supplied. Furniture manufacturers will often have regular fortnightly or monthly
delivery runs to customers in specific parts of the country,
and lead times are built into the order process to tie in
with these deliveries to make them cost-effective. However, for the majority of small items and one-off sales
over long distances, it is seldom profitable to use direct
deliveries.

- What are the alternatives? For small items and infrequent
orders, mail order is often the easiest method. For high-
value or fragile items, contract deliveries (Business Post,
TNT, UPS, Amtrak, etc.), which use a network of international and local depots offering an overnight service
throughout the country, are relatively cheap and efficient.
By making prompt and efficient deliveries to your customers, they aim to retain you as one of their customers,
so the interest is mutual. Consider the cost of running just
one delivery vehicle for a year: the capital outlay and depre-
ciation, interest on finance, road tax, insurance, breakdown
cover, fuel, tyres, repairs and maintenance, delays caused
by traffic jams and breakdowns, hiring replacement vehicles, the drivers' wages, their national insurance, sickness
and holiday pay, cover for lateness and absence, the cost
of the supervisor who plans the deliveries and organizes
and administers the vehicles. It might pay to total up all of
these costs and then divide them by the number of pack-
ages or items delivered by that vehicle in a year. How, then,
does the unit cost of those compare with the postal or contract delivery alternative?

- What sort of transport do I need? The obvious answer is
to match the vehicle to the weight, size, volume and numbers of items being delivered. Usually, the larger the capacity (volume or payload) of the vehicle, the lower the unit
cost of the deliveries, although the final decision may also
be affected by where the goods are to be delivered and how
they will get there. Consider Case Study 2.

Kent and Sussex Ales was a small real ale, beer and mineral wholesaler supplying pubs, clubs and restaurants in a relatively rural area. It currently used three transit-type vans for deliveries. Most of these involved just two or three casks of beer delivered to pubs typically spaced about five miles apart in country areas using minor roads. Some journeys involved round trips of 80 miles per day. A few customers (about 10 per cent) placed larger orders of eight or more casks.

As the business grew, a decision had to be made about acquiring additional delivery capacity. Two options were considered:

Option 1: To sell one of the existing transit vans (payload 1.5 tonnes) and buy a 7-tonne truck (payload 4 tonnes), and to employ an additional driver/delivery man.

This option offered more capacity overall (an additional 1.0 tonne or about eighteen small casks of beer) and would save on road tax, insurance, MOT costs, etc. The fuel consumption was slightly higher but because of the extra volume and payload, the larger vehicle could undertake longer journeys. Loading and unloading was slightly slower due to the curtain-sided access.

Option 2: To buy an additional transit-type van (payload 1.5 tonnes) and to employ an additional driver. This option would incur extra capital expenditure and overhead costs (tax, insurance, MOT, etc.) compared with Option 1, amounting to some £8000 per year.

The larger vehicle was the obvious choice on the grounds of cost savings, and appeared to be more efficient as it could handle larger quantities of goods and make longer journeys. It raised the overall delivery payload of all vehicles to 7 tonnes, whereas Option 2 offered only 6 tonnes. However, a four-week trial of the options using rented vehicles threw up several major issues:

- First, the majority of pub customers were not early risers and wanted deliveries between 9.00 a.m. and 3.00 p.m., when they closed for the afternoon, and the longer journeys could not be fitted within that time scale.

- Second, until the larger van was tried, the drivers had not realized that most of the short cuts used to ensure deliveries used narrow country lanes, many of which had width or weight restrictions that the larger truck could not meet.

- Third, by planning small van routes carefully so that one of the four vans was retained for closer deliveries, the short-haul van was capable of a second daily run, which made up for the lower delivery capacity of the four small vans.

The extra capital and operating costs of Option 2 were more than outweighed by the flexibility gained, and in keeping the customers happy by delivering on time. However, in a more urban area with closer delivery points, better roads and possibly larger delivery drops, the reverse might have been true.

- Should I lease or buy my vehicles? In the early days when a business is first established profits are small if any, regular outgoings must be minimized, and there is usually a preference to maximize the tangible assets shown on the balance sheet. For this purpose, hire purchase is ideal, as once the initial down payment is made the regular payments are relatively low, and the net value of the purchase can be shown on the balance sheet as the buyer will eventually own it. The less attractive tax relief offered by the capital allowance system is not seen as a problem as taxable profits are usually modest. However, by the time an owner-manager has consolidated the business and is thinking of expansion, this situation should have changed. With trading profits coming in there is less need for assets to be shown on the balance sheet, but there is a need to minimize tax liabilities, and here leasing is a better option. As the business does not and never will own the leased vehicles, they cannot be treated as an asset, but on the other hand, they do constitute a tax-deductible operating expense of the business. In simple terms, then, hire purchase is a better option than a bank loan, as it does not have to be secured on anything more than the purchased item itself; but for companies in profit, leasing is more tax efficient than hire purchase.

● Are my current information systems performing to meet my needs? This is not just an issue in information technology, it is also about the basics of organizing your administrative systems, i.e. can you find something when you need it? There are some records that must be kept for tax or VAT purposes and others like customer records that are important for the running of the business. However, there is other information sitting in your filing cabinet and taking up space, that you will never use again. When did you last review your information systems to determine what information is essential and what is just clutter, out-of-date trade brochures, etc.? The point of all this is that if you are planning a substantial expansion of your business, then the administrative systems will need to be able to support that growth.

**Administration, IT and communications**

● So, where are the shortfalls in the current systems? Do you waste time because you have trouble finding papers that have been filed? Do you have piles of papers waiting to be filed? Are you keeping paper records when electronic data storage would be more efficient? With the cost of PCs currently lower than they have ever been, there is no longer any excuse for cumbersome paper-based systems for anything but the most basic business, but the use of computerized accounting, database and word-processing systems does require a modicum of discipline. In particular, the accessibility they offer in terms of fast and accurate data recovery will only work if data are backed up regularly and stored securely.

● The type of electronic data storage and communication systems you choose should not just be determined by your own current and prospective needs, they should also be considered in relation to those of your customers. What preferred systems of communication do the customers use, e.g. telephone, fax, e-mail, etc.? Can you be sure that they can all make contact with you easily? How many orders might you be losing because customers cannot fax or e-mail their requirements to you, or speak to anything other than an answerphone? What is the cost to you of those lost orders in an average year? That is a hard question to answer, but you only have to lose one order each week to make a big hole in your annual profits, and once a customer is lost it is much harder to win them back. In this context, it is not too hard to justify a modest investment in computing and communications systems.

## Raw materials, resale stock and packaging

Issues of stock management are of less interest to service-provider businesses, but they can be critical to retailing, wholesaling or manufacturing firms, particularly if the firm is in a competitive market where profit margins are tight, or where it has adopted a strategic policy of cost leadership. It does not take a great deal of lost or damaged stock to knock a big hole in the firm's profit. For example, if you are buying items in at £80 to resell them for £100, then on the face of it for every lost or damaged item you will need to sell an extra four just to cover the cost of the lost item. In reality, the figure is higher as there will be variable costs (distribution expenses, etc.) associated with each of those sales. Efficient stock management is important, so we will look at a few of the questions that must be asked.

- What improvements could be made? First, you have to identify the problems by asking the question: am I managing my stocks properly? There are a multitude of things which can go wrong in handling stocks: loss through damage or theft, waste caused by poor rotation or over-stocking beyond use-by dates, over-purchasing resulting in too much working capital tied up in stock, too much stock, re-order systems. Problems can also occur in paperwork systems, e.g. where incoming stock is not checked against delivery notes, or the quantities, prices and discounts are not checked against the suppliers' invoices. Outgoing stocks must also be monitored, particularly where urgent deliveries or collections are involved outside of normal working hours. It is very easy to help a customer out by staying open late for a collection, but will the accounting system pick up that collection and invoice the customer for it. If the stocks are eminently 'desirable', e.g. booze, cigarettes or electrical consumer goods, be watchful of slippage, i.e. theft by warehouse or distribution staff whose ingenuity at theft will certainly outstrip their initiative and creativity demonstrated within their regular jobs.

- Am I managing my purchases properly? It pays to carry out a periodic review of the terms of trade offered by suppliers, e.g. the relative discounts offered by various suppliers, delivery charges incurred, credit terms, reliability of supply and delivery, etc. Very often, this review is best carried out together with suppliers, and with a bit of imagination or lateral thinking it can generate benefits for both parties. For example, there may be an optimum order or delivery size for the supplier that will result in cost savings that can be shared by both parties – 'if you can take a whole truck load in one drop, I can give you a better unit price'. It is easy to forget that our suppliers are in business to make a profit as well as we are, so the relationship has to be mutually acceptable. It is as much in the supplier's interest for you to make a profit and to continue buying, as it is for the supplier to make a profit and stay in business to supply you.

- How would I describe my relationship with my suppliers? Perhaps a more appropriate approach would be to ask the question – what do my suppliers really think of me? Would they describe me as a good customer? Do they welcome my orders or am I tolerated as a necessary evil? Do they always have to chase me for payment or can they rely on me to pay on time? There is much to be said for sustainable supplier relationships, and reliability and quality service can prove more important in the long term than squeezing the last per cent of discount from them. The relationship should work both ways, so that if you need a bit of leeway, e.g. a few extra days credit to cover a cash-flow problem, there should be no embarrassment in asking. Similarly, the suppliers should feel able to ask you for payment a few days early if they have similar problems.

- Over-packaging, particularly on food products, has become a major problem in recent years. The average Kit-Kat bought in a multi-pack at Tesco will usually have three layers, and sometimes four, and the British government is now forcing businesses to have a positive policy of recycling a large proportion of packaging. Can I reduce my packaging costs then? This will depend on what the packaging is for, e.g. to protect the goods during consignment, or to sell the products to the end-user, but as a part of the stock management review process, the question must be raised: is all of the packaging on my products really necessary?

*Reference*

Butler, D. (2000). *Business Planning – A Guide to Business Start-Up*. Butterworth-Heinemann.

# Chapter 5 Developing
Chapter 5
Chapter 5 a sales and
marketing
strategy

In Chapter 1, we discussed the headless chicken syndrome, wherein small businesses have a tendency, in the early stages of their existence, to chase all sales opportunities that come their way irrespective of profitability, on the assumption that any sales that make a contribution towards their overheads must be good for the business. In consequence, they often expend a great deal of effort chasing low-margin sales when a more planned and directed approach could have resulted in more profit for less effort. As the business matures the effort is directed towards the profitable sales opportunities, but such opportunities are usually limited because of competition in the market. If the business is to expand and develop in the long term, it has therefore to focus on the market segments where it can use its strengths to the full.

This chapter will look at some contemporary ideas about the strategic marketing audit, the process of identifying suitable market segments and the production of the strategic marketing plan, and how these apply to small and developing firms. The issues that are examined here relate to Units B1, B2, B4 and B5 of the Revised Business Development Standards.

## The marketing audit

The first stage in preparing your business for expansion is to carry out a review of the marketing processes presently in use, identifying areas of strengths and weaknesses, current spare capacity and/or overload, and in particular any major

76

problems that need to be addressed. Some of the relevant issues will hopefully already have been picked up during the strategic analysis of the business.

Hooley et al. (1998) propose that the starting point of the marketing audit should be to examine the organizational assets of the business, covering the finances, physical assets, people, operations, intellectual property (patents and copyrights, etc.), systems and marketing assets. Drummond and Ensor (1999) focus on the last of these as being particularly significant to marketing strategy, the marketing assets, which fall into four categories:

- First, the customer-based assets are those which are important in the eyes of the customer: the image and reputation of the business in the marketplace, any brands which the business owns that are strong enough to generate customer loyalty (and therefore a potential competitive advantage over rival businesses). The customers' perceptions of the business as a market leader or brand leader are also significant in that, in the case of fast-moving consumer goods, such perceptions can generate prime locations within retail outlets. They also mention the country of origin as being relevant, quoting as an example the German car manufacturers BMW and Mercedes. Whilst this may be relevant to the international motor trade, I am not so sure of its importance to small firms unless they are producing or selling premium goods for the top end of the consumer market. It is certainly less applicable to service industries. The key features to focus on are the unique features of products and services which distinguish them from the competition, whether it be price, quality, design, or a combination of these.

- The size and strength of the distribution network in key geographical areas is seen as a key asset. This is not just an issue of the size of the area covered, or its depth of coverage, but the speed and efficiency in which the business can respond to its customers. The other aspect of distribution is whether or not the firm has any influence or control over the distribution network. The example quoted by Drummond and Ensor (p. 53) is that of Coca-Cola using its global influence to keep the relatively small Scottish Irn-Bru out of MacDonalds restaurants. As a case in point, this illustrates well one of the major problems facing small firms in large international markets. Even where the barriers to market entry can be overcome, it is very seldom the case that small firms can achieve any degree of market control, except of course with the approval of the large global organizations.

- Cost structure advantages such as economies of scale or the application of technology can provide valuable internal assets to a business, although in small firms the economies of scale are much less likely to be as significant as the ability to make use of innovative technology. Equally, the information systems used for market research are likely to be less significant to small firms, apart perhaps from those working in the information technology markets.

- The fourth type of assets are described as alliance-based, because they involve the advantages gained from external relationships with other organizations, and this is one area where small firms can potentially score highly. For example, many small firms gain access to larger markets via partnerships or contracts with other distributors or suppliers in those markets, sometimes involving exclusive supply agreements with major players in the market. Such relationships can also involve savings from shared product development. In this respect, suppliers of Venture Capital can count as an asset in terms of both the networking opportunities and the management expertise they can offer to their siblings.

Can you, then, identify any of these internal assets which may exist within your business, or are there any possible areas which could be exploited for the future? Are there any other internal factors that could be regarded as internal assets, such as any specialist marketing knowledge or expertise relating to the firm's customers and markets? Most important, having identified your internal assets, are you making them work for you to their full potential?

Kotler et al. (1999) outlined a five-stage model for the marketing audit process which can help managers of both large and small firms to carry out an audit of their own organizations. The model is really designed to challenge any comfortable assumptions that all is well in the marketing context, as it highlights each of the possible areas where problems could have crept in over a period of time, since the marketing policies were formulated or last reviewed. This is especially pertinent to small firms, where policy reviews are not automatic, often because of the singular and sometimes autocratic role of the owner-manager as the primary decision-maker.

- The Marketing Strategy Audit looks at the compatibility of current marketing activity with the overall marketing objectives of the organization, and if sufficient resources have been allocated to allow the objectives to be achieved. Do the activities fit with the strategies or have they diverged over a period of time? One would think that with the more specialized management resources available to big companies this would be less likely to happen than in a small business, where the owner-manager may be more readily distracted from original policies. Have your marketing activities inadvertently diverged from the original plans over the past year or so? Are the differences just minor or has there been a major change in direction, and what impact has that had on sales volumes and revenues? What were the reasons for the change? Do the current activities now need to be brought into line with the overall strategic objectives of the business?

- The Marketing Structures Audit looks at the role of the marketing function within the organization as a whole, its representation within the management and decision-making process, and its relationships with other functional areas of the business. In theory, the sales and marketing functions should be of prime importance to the owner-manager, as they are the lifelines of the business, but in many small firms they are relegated to a secondary position. This is a particularly common occurrence if the owner-manager comes from a manufacturing or technical background, when the 'marketing' (or more often just the advertising) is often delegated to a secretary to arrange. Conversely, owner-managers from a sales background tend to place a strong emphasis on marketing, although with a strong awareness of the importance of the product itself in the marketing mix; the need for technical expertise is not relegated to a lower priority in the same manner. Where, then, does the marketing role fit within your business, and have you got the balance right?

- The Marketing Systems Audit looks at the planning and control systems used, and new product development. Are you able to monitor and evaluate the returns achieved by sales and marketing activities, for example in terms of enquiries or actual sales generated by an advertising campaign, or by the regular activities of sales staff? Does the product development policy of the business follow from market information and research, or from the inspirations of the owner-manager and technical staff? There is nothing wrong with the latter, but the former does a great deal to validate its potential benefits and to guide it in the right direction. The systems audit should also include a review of the market research activities and capabilities of the organization, in particular with an examination of the depth to which research is carried out. Market research is not an activity that comes easy to many owner-managers and there can be a tendency, often driven by experience in a particular industry or service, to assume that there is little more to be learnt beyond that which the owner-manager already knows. This is more important prior to a period of growth or development, especially when diversifying into new markets, as it is all too easy to underestimate the barriers to market entry because they have not been sufficiently researched. For example, there may be a big market out there waiting for you, but how much of it is tied up in long-term contracts with major competitors whose size and economies of scale enable them to control and manipulate prices to keep out newcomers.

- The Productivity Audit looks at the contributions made by the various products or services offered, their individual profit/cost ratios, and the cost-effectiveness of the various distribution channels and markets. Do you know which of your products or services (a) generate the biggest overall contribution towards profit and overheads for the business, (b) generate the best profit margins, and (c) fail to cover their costs? Do you know which of your lines of distribution contribute the biggest profit to the business? Are any of the markets in which you operate actually losing you money? This analysis can provide useful data about products or markets on which to focus, and others to avoid or withdraw from in the future. Forget the fancy title, this particular audit process should be regarded as an aspect of basic good housekeeping, as most small businesses have the necessary data available to them to extract this information, although they do not always make time or take the trouble to find the answers to these questions.

- The Marketing Functions Audit is a way of reviewing the marketing mix (product, price, place and promotion, etc.), to investigate its ongoing effectiveness. Are there any factors that have changed the relative significance of any of the components, e.g. an aggressive pricing policy or advertising campaign by a major rival? Has the demand for the product(s) changed at all? Most important of all, to link in with the strategic objectives of the business, what changes in the marketing mix are now needed? This

81

last question will reflect the decisions made about the strategic options faced by the business (cost leadership, diversification, market focus, etc.), as it will tell you how far off the mark the business actually is.

## Market segmentation

In the previous section, we mentioned the importance of comprehensive market research, and one of the key focal points of marker research should be to identify the individual market segments which constitute the market as a whole. People do not simply drive cars, they drive saloons, estates, coupes, convertibles, sports models, roadsters, off-roaders, etc. The sports car options start at the modest and very basic self-build Caterham kit-cars, through MGs and Jaguars, through to more expensive Porches, to the top-of-the-range Lamborghinis and customized Ferraris. Every type of car and every price variant of each type constitutes a different market segment within which it is broadly possible to stereotype the potential customers according to certain common characteristics, such as income, type of employment, social class, family composition, etc. The average engineer, social worker, salesman, school teacher or college lecturer might aspire to owning a three- or four-bedroom house and a fairly new middle-range saloon car, but short of a lottery win that person could not hope to achieve the lifestyle and associated expensive cars enjoyed by Premier League footballers.

The purpose of identifying market segments is to evaluate and select those in which the business can achieve some differential advantage over its competitors. This does not mean the firm has to focus on just one or two segments, rather that it can build up a portfolio of segments that complement each other in terms of generating income and contribution to overhead coverage and profit. Put simply, we are trying to identify various groups or types of customers who share common characteristics, or similar patterns of demand, so that we can focus our sales and marketing effort towards them. The market research enables you to select those that offer you the biggest

**Table 5.1** Market segmentation example for a private security business

| Type of Organization | Examples | Contract Value per annum | Profit Margin | Service Criteria | Financial or Quality Motivation | Service Requirements | Percentage of Total Business |
|---|---|---|---|---|---|---|---|
| Public sector, large | Govt. depts, schools, local authorities, hospitals | £100k–£300k | 10%–20% | On-going reliability | Cost motivated within specified standards | Regular full-time days + night patrols | 30% |
| Private companies | Office based service, and high-tech companies | £200k | 15%–25% | On-going reliability, and security sensitive | Professional service at reasonable price | Full-time day and night staff All staff screened. | 50% |
| Private individuals | Owners of large private homes | £10k–£15k | 30% | Reliability. Honest staff | Professional service but value for money | Regular mobile patrols, plus full-time cover in owner's absence | 15% |
| Major public functions and events | Rock concerts, VIP visits and personal protection | £2k–£20k | 60% | Available at short notice, and anti-social hours | Discreet and efficient high quality service, with minimal disruption | Round-the-clock security and surveillance | 5% |

potential in terms of sales volume or profit, in relation to the effort expended in achieving those sales. By virtue of the fact that they will have differential characteristics and criteria for buying, they will require different approaches, i.e. marketing mixes. Table 5.1 shows an example of segmentation prepared for a small private security business. This shows examples of the types of customer, the typical value and profit margins of their contracts, their service criteria and requirements, their motivation in terms of price or quality of service, and finally the proportion of the firm's total sales that are likely to be derived from each type of contract.

Drummond and Ensor (1999, pp. 108–9) propose that market segments should be assessed in terms of both the market attractiveness of the various segments, and the ability of the firm to supply the needs of the particular segments. For the small business, this raises a number of issues:

- Should the firm focus on larger opportunities to gain economies of scale and to justify greater investment in market development, but run the risk of heavier competition from rivals, or should it focus on smaller niche segments that will not readily attract the unwanted attention of our rivals?

- What are the opportunities for growth within the segments? Are we looking at good profitable opportunities, or mature or even declining markets? The former would be preferable, but again might also attract the attention of competitors. The latter, although less attractive, could still offer good short-term profits.

- Which of our competitors are already active in the segments, and will there be enough potential profit within them to justify the investment incurred in breaking into the market segments? Conversely, if we move into a segment where there is unsatisfied demand, what barriers or costs are there to stop our rivals moving in alongside, and reducing our profits?

- How sensitive is the population of the segment to price? Price sensitivity may mean working on low profit margins, but less sensitivity could give an opportunity for good profits, so long as we do not attract too much attention from our rivals.

- What is the pattern of demand within the segment? It is unusual for any market to have a totally level and consistent demand, as most markets are influenced in some way by seasonal factors (weather, Christmas or festival dates, holiday seasons, etc.).

- What are the possibilities that a particular niche market will become a target for new alternative or substitute products that could render ours obsolete? Can we afford this risk? Are we in a position to develop innovative products ourselves?

## The strategic marketing plan

The above questions will help to provide the criteria by which we can evaluate the relative potential of the various optional market segments that are available. If the chosen segments are compatible with our overall strategic objectives, we can move on to define the marketing plan, i.e. the policies and tactics we will use to address these market opportunities, and the competencies we will employ to gain an advantage over our competitors. The plan should develop a marketing mix for each of the target market segments that will make full use and advantage of the strengths of the business and its marketing resources. This is the process of getting the right product or service, of the right quality, to the place where the customer wants it, at the right price, and using the right methods of advertising and promotion to optimize profits along the way.

The strategic analysis and the resultant chosen options should have determined the organization's policies for the pricing strategy of the products or services, as well as the plans for future product development in terms of the focus or diversification of the product range. The subsequent marketing audit and segmentation of the market will have determined the target market and its customers, and will assist in making decisions about our position in the markets in terms of our strengths, public image and brand awareness, as well as our ability to respond to changes in the markets, to develop new and innovative products or service advantages, etc. Remember, what we are looking at here are the strategies with which we will implement the overall policies and objectives of the business. Those strategies should complement the objectives rather than diverge from them, or result in activities that compete with each other for limited marketing resources. In the case of the marketing plan, this means that the strategies should be formulated in conjunction with the plans of other functional areas within the business (production, finance, sales, etc.) and not in isolation. This is to ensure that their respective activities are complementary, do not detract from each other or do not compete with each other for limited company resources.

Having then covered the Price, Product and Place aspects of the marketing mix, the next chapter will look at the Promotion, i.e. the long-term policies and tactics that will promote and sell the products or services, and the new opportunities currently emerging to achieve these policies.

*References*

Drummond, G. and Ensor, J. (1999). *Strategic Marketing Planning and Control*. Butterworth-Heinemann.

Hooley, G. H., Saunders, J. A. and Piercy, N. F. (1998). *Marketing Strategy and Competitive Positioning*, 2nd Edn. Prentice Hall.

Kotler, P., Armstrong, G., Saunders, J. and Wong, V. (1999). *Principles of Marketing*, 2nd European Edn. Prentice Hall.

# Chapter 6   Expanding the market

Chapter 6
Chapter 6

The first part of this chapter is concerned with the tactical aspects of the marketing plan for the business. The Product, Price and Place aspects of the marketing mix are essentially the policy decisions covered in the previous chapter, but the Promotion aspects (achieving the sales) are more tactical in that they relate to the methods that will be used to project and present the other three aspects to the market and the customers. In particular, there is a need to distinguish the 'marketing' aspects of promotion from the 'sales' aspects. Advertising and promotion create interest in a business or its products and services, and in the case of direct sales organizations, it is also the sales mechanism that takes the orders. However, for the majority of businesses, the marketing and promotion activities alone do not always generate sales orders. There needs to be a supporting mechanism in the form of staff who are actively selling to customers, or an order-taking and processing system, to convert interest and enquiries into actual orders.

The chapter will also examine some of the issues associated with exporting and e-commerce, two increasingly overlapping areas. The first of these is an obvious potential opportunity for any firm considering expansion. The second is a subject that no modern business can afford to ignore, as Internet marketing offers small firms the opportunity to break into wider geographical and export markets hitherto inaccessible to them. This chapter relates to Units A2, B1, B2, B3, B4 and B5 of the revised Business Development Standards.

It is very easy, when running a small business, to go from year to year using the same tried and tested methods of advertising and promotion without giving thought either to whether or not they are still achieving satisfactory results or to new or alternative options. The monitoring of sales and promotional activities should be an ongoing process, e.g. in terms of enquiries and actual sales per advertisement, of numbers of sales calls per day, conversion rates per sales call, the revenue sales volumes and profit margins generated by each sales person, etc. Sadly, this monitoring is often overwhelmed and subsumed by other business pressures until suddenly a major problem is identified. Sometimes the problem goes unnoticed until perhaps a salesman leaves and the replacement person swamps the business with orders, making the owner-manager suddenly aware that the former employee was ineffective and that this had gone unnoticed. So, the point at which the owner-manager is looking for growth and development within the business should also be the point at which the efficacy of the sales and promotion activities are reviewed, as they need to be fully efficient to facilitate that new growth. The review process requires the owner-manager to consider a further range of questions:

- What methods of advertising and promotion are currently being used? Does the business use a wide range of methods or does it just rely on one or two proven options? Has it chosen those methods because they are the most appropriate for the needs of the business, or were they simply the most convenient at the time?

- Are the current methods satisfactory, i.e. do they optimize the sales opportunities for the business? Are they cost-effective in terms of the profit they generate in comparison with the actual costs incurred? Are they generating the levels of sales expected of them? What evidence is there to verify the answers to these questions? For example, if we choose a particular form of advertising, say adverts in local newspapers, we would expect the profit gained from the additional sales which result

**Developing an advertising and promotion strategy**

from the advertising to more than outweigh the cost of the advertising, otherwise it has been a failure. If there were a choice of more than one local newspaper in which we can advertise, we would need to monitor the adverts in order to determine which of the two gives us the best results. This could be measured in terms of the number of enquiries that follow each advert, and/or the number of sales that results from those enquiries. We should also be monitoring these on an ongoing basis to identify seasonal fluctuations or other factors which may be affecting the response levels, so that, for example, we do not advertise at those times of year when we know demand will fall. If the business offers a multiple range of products or services, then it will be necessary to monitor the effectiveness of each form of promotion against each product, as particular methods will prove more efficient in selling to some market segments than others, and the business needs to be able to identify the best method to reach each type of customer for each product or service. This is just good basic common sense market research.

- Will the same methods be compatible with the plans for expansion? If the plans for expansion involve moving into new markets or diversifying product ranges, then the answer to this question will almost certainly be no. It is imperative, therefore, that you do not just assume that because your favourite sales and marketing methods have worked in the past, they will still work for your new services or new market segment customers. In the earlier chapters, we talked about identifying tactics that will enable us to implement the strategic objectives. Part of that process involves defining suitable methods of advertising and promotion that will enable the business to hit its sales targets in the new market segments, or for its new product lines.

- What actual methods of sales and/or promotion will be needed for the future? No business can rely on its reputation or on word of mouth recommendation alone to sell its goods or services, and it is rare that any single method of promotion will be adequate, so we are usually looking for a combination of methods from the most popular available:

– Media advertising using television, radio, posters and hoardings, etc. can reach large proportions of the buying public quite easily, and are particularly good for raising and maintaining brand awareness amongst household products, and for encouraging the public to buy those products. They are, however, expensive and have relatively little use in selling specialist services to specific parts of the market. The television adverts might tell me what is the best beer to drink or crisps to eat while I am watching football, but they will not tell me who is the best supplier of contract catering in my locality.

– Publications: local for local sales and services; a double-glazing firm does not want to be travelling all over the country if it can get enough trade within a fifty-mile radius. National advertising for national markets, e.g. a company selling stair-lifts for the elderly will probably need to trade nationally to ensure it can get sufficient business to cover overheads and make a healthy profit, whereas to just trade on a county-wide basis would risk failure. Specialist publications are ideal for niche markets: suppliers of pigeon food for racing pigeons advertise in the *Pigeon Fancier* or *Fur and Feather* magazines, whilst purveyors of the kinky stuff prefer to advertise in *Leather and Rubber Weekly* – they might sound similar but there is a radical difference in the readership! You pay the money and take your choice of the one that suits your market.

– Employed sales staff: there are two main options here, to train up existing staff, which can be cheaper for younger businesses, or buy in or recruit already trained staff from competitors. Recruiting experienced sales staff tends to cost much more as you are paying for a track record of sales skills, experience in the industry, and usually a ready-made list of contacts and potential customers. The extra cost is often justified by the more rapid returns through increased sales, but there is always the risk that poached staff can be poached back by the offer of higher rewards elsewhere. 'Home-grown' sales staff, if properly rewarded, can often prove the most loyal in the long term.

– Sales agents can provide a source of skills, experience and relevant industrial knowledge. They are relatively cheap, usually being paid a basic retainer fee plus commission on results, but being independent they are not under your direct control, and you may find at times that there is a conflict between your priorities and those of the other organizations that use them.

– Franchises: the features that attract potential franchisees to a franchise opportunity in the first place are normally associated with the pre-existing brand image and reputation of the franchise opportunity. Classic examples are household names such as Body Shop, McDonalds, and more recent arrivals such as Starbucks coffee and Kall-Kwik printing.

– Licensed products: where the owner of the patent or copyright of a particular product issues licences for other businesses to produce and supply that product into specified market areas. There are normally only four reasons why a business would contemplate selling licences to allow other firms to promote and distribute their products: a lack of capital to allow them to expand the market themselves, to break into an export market with the minimum of effort and investment, to stave off the risk of unauthorized copies of the product, or as the result of an offer too good to refuse.

– Internet: the major growth area for cheap coverage of potentially worldwide markets. This opportunity is

91

examined in more detail below, but with the rapid growth of e-commerce and the Internet as a source of product information, this is becoming a means of promotion which must invariably sit alongside all others in the future.

– Telesales activities as a means of selling have expanded at an enormous rate in the last five years. There are two basic formats: the telesales answering services that respond to sales advertisements on TV and in the newspapers, such as SAGA Holidays and Direct Line Insurance, and the cold-calling telesales typical of replacement window and conservatory suppliers. What always amazes me about the latter is that they always call you, without fail, when you are in the middle of an evening meal – it is almost as if they have some secret device which links their telephone service with the cooker in your home! Cold-calling telesales is very much a numbers game, requiring a large number of calls to generate a few enquiries, and even less actual sales, but the frequency with which we receive such calls at home must be indicative of its cost-effectiveness.

Remember, the criteria for selecting the most appropriate method or combination of methods of advertising and promotion should not just focus on comparative costs or potential returns on outlay, they must also ensure that the advertising and promotion policies complement the overall development strategies of the business.

## Selling and exporting abroad

What is it that turns the heads of owner-managers to think about exporting? Paliwoda and Thomas (1998, p. 105) argue that, in general, this is rarely the result of planned or extensive market research. Sometimes it is an order or enquiry from a foreign country that arrives unexpectedly and prompts the sudden realization that life (and business) exists beyond the

Straits of Dover. Once the order has been met and the basic export procedures are in place, it is an obvious next step to make further use of these by searching for more export opportunities. In other cases, it may be the prospect of low-cost or low-risk entry into markets that are proving hard to penetrate, or are already saturated, in the home country.

The export markets may present an opportunity to expand production of current product lines, and to grow the business without the capital investment costs that may be incurred by a strategy of product diversification. This does not, however, imply that exporting is a low-cost option, as the costs of developing an export market can be substantial, in terms of preliminary market research and sales effort, and the funds tied up in goods in transit, or when payment is awaited from foreign distributors. In particular, the costs of replacing or servicing faulty goods can quickly wipe out profit margins, so the move into exporting should not be considered lightly.

The potential exporter must also make decisions about the extent of the involvement the business will have in the foreign markets, and a number of options exist here:

- If the business decides to utilize spare capacity at the home base, and transport the goods abroad, decisions still need to be made about the sales and distribution networks that will be used:

  - Do we set up a complete sales and distribution network from scratch, thus incurring substantial initial outlay and ongoing overhead costs, possibly in a market where the true levels of demand for the goods are not yet assured? This could be both a high-cost and high-risk strategy if we do not have good market knowledge and established contacts.

  - Do we set up a foreign base but use sales agents who have better local market knowledge, as well as established contacts with potential users or outlets? This gives a measure of control over the issue of goods, but still incurs some capital outlay and overheads.

- Do we simply supply a foreign agent or wholesaler who would then undertake the whole sales and distribution process on our behalf? In terms of capital outlay and operating costs this is the cheapest option, but it does mean that once the goods have been despatched abroad, we have no control over them, and we are totally reliant on the efficiency and honesty of the agent.

● If there is inadequate spare production capacity at home, it may be more cost-effective to set up production abroad, generating savings on the cost of transport or carriage between countries, and possibly achieving lower production costs with local labour.

- Do we set up a new production facility with all of the capital and development costs? In some foreign countries, this might attract subsidies or incentives, although in others it may be necessary to grease a few palms to avoid problems or delays. Either way, capital costs may be well beyond the resources of a small firm without outside help.

- Do we sub-contract the licence to an established manufacturer in a similar industry (if such exists)? An alternative option might be a joint venture with a local manufacturer, but such ventures can present a great deal of risk and exposure, especially if there are problems or disagreements when local courts may favour the home-player.

- Do we franchise or license the products for local production? This can be a practical proposition if the business holds patents or copyrights, although there are always potential problems of enforcing these on foreign soil. In some oriental countries there can also be problems arising from unauthorized copying of patented goods, resulting in the market being swamped with cheaply produced copies.

- A less common but often cheaper and more practical option is for the would-be exporter to join a consortium of other exporters that produce complementary products for the same markets. This can generate savings in shipping costs, storage, sales and distribution costs, whilst giving access to established distribution networks, and utilizing established or shared administrative systems. The hardest problem here is in making the initial contacts with other exporters, but there are government agencies and advisory bodies that exist just to assist with such problems.

The export business does offer the potential of high and sustainable long-term profits, but it is also riddled with risks, obstacles and potential problems for small firms:

- Identification of potential markets and customers. Apart from the practical difficulties and expense of carrying out market research from a distance, in many cases the data simply do not exist. In addition, small firms often have limited resources, both in terms of finance and management time, and invariably they also have little or no expertise in exporting. Paliwoda and Thomas (1998, p. 106) state that, in consequence, the small firms tend to spend relatively little money on market research, and to focus their sales effort on trade fairs and exhibitions, and personal visits to major customers. Other than this, the majority of small firms seem to prefer to work through agents.

- The actual selection of reliable distributors or agents can be a problem in that although there are sources of information about available export agents through various government agencies and business support organizations, it is much harder to obtain information about the quality, honesty and efficiency of the various agents. This may sound a bit xenophobic, but from the perspective of most owner-managers, there is an obvious risk in supplying goods on credit to a person they may not even have met, who is thousands of miles away, speaks a different native language, has a differing cultural view of life, with possible different business objectives, and an unknown reputation. These are the same owner-managers who are often reluctant to trust their own secretaries to do the daily banking in their hometown!

- When dealing with foreign countries there are the obvious barriers of language, culture and pace of life, where 'urgent' means 'some time this week', or where families take priority over business. The cultural differences often prove frustrating and hard to comprehend, but the problem is compounded when they cannot easily be discussed due to different languages, and profit is at stake. The average owner-manager's time is at a premium, and foreign travel is both expensive and time-consuming, so it can be exasperating to reach the end of a long journey only to find your destination is closed for three days due to a local religious festival!

- The economic aspects of foreign trade must not be ignored. Fluctuations in exchange rates between the dates of sale and dates of payment can often wipe out or minimize profit margins. Some countries still operate trade tariffs, taxing or restricting imports, and others have restrictions on the amounts of currency that can be taken out of the country. It is no good having a huge and profitable market opportunity if you cannot bring that profit back to your home country, or if the currency in which you are paid has little exchange value.

- There is also the need to establish letters of credit from reputable banks to ensure that your customers or agents will pay you, and this in itself can be a time-consuming process, especially as some banks have a minimum transaction level which may be above the average sale value of small exporters. Fortunately, there are some government agencies and other bodies that can assist in these matters:

- The Department of Trade and Industry in London has an Export Market Information Centre (EMIC) which can be a useful source of data and statistics for various world markets, and can provide information on international trade fairs and events. Its Export Marketing Research Scheme (EMRS) also offers advice on how to get market research information for different products in different world regions. It also has information on country profiles and directories for various parts of the world.

- The Export Credit Guarantee Department (ECGD) can offer advice on credit guarantees and contacts with specialists in various parts of the world, but is primarily geared towards the needs of larger exporters.

- The English Export Finance Association in Rochdale is more suited to small firms as it handles smaller credit transactions than mainstream banks will normally touch.

- The British Standards Institution offers a service called Technical Help to Exporters, which can provide data concerning rules and regulations in foreign countries. Similarly, H. M. Customs and Excise can provide information on UK regulations affecting exports out of the UK. In addition, there are a number of trade associations and national export organizations that offer export advice to members, including the British Exporters Association and the British Chambers of Commerce, which can be accessed via the Internet.

The rapid growth of e-commerce in recent years has turned aspects of conventional marketing theory upside down, the Internet itself now being the Place part of the marketing mix, in a worldwide rather than local context, and the distribution systems being postal or contract delivery services rather than direct deliveries by the producer to the customer. Because of the Internet, the physical location of the manufacturer or supplier is of much less importance, but the quality and efficiency of the communications system is now of paramount importance. In effect, the user-friendly website, the facility for secure payment, the convenience of armchair shopping and the promise of prompt delivery have become the new customer service system. The Internet has streamlined mail order purchase systems, particularly for CDs and videos etc., because in the time it previously took to post an order and cheque to the supplier, the goods have now been delivered. It has opened up the market size or customer potential for small firms supplying niche markets, and it has offered an affordable system of advertising and selling in those markets, when the cost of conventional sales activities would have prohibited entry into those markets.

*Internet marketing*

In many respects, small firms have responded better to the new opportunities of e-commerce than their larger counterparts. Big companies make good use of the Internet to dissipate knowledge and information, and to communicate with their global customers, but websites are used more for advertising and information sources, rather than to generate direct sales. The big companies also tend to opt for more grandiose websites with colour photographs of impressive premises, products or achievements, which although they look good, do tend to slow down the whole process of Internet access. In contrast, small firms have been fast to recognize that what their customers want is rapid access to information, the ability to place orders in a financially secure environment, and to be able to monitor the progress of those orders during delivery. Businesses that were previously restricted to small local markets have suddenly become international traders, and both sales and profits have grown fast. The overall implication of this is that for the small business wishing to develop and expand, e-commerce represents a monumental opportunity to engage a huge marketplace at costs that were previously inconceivably low. This is also one way in which the small fry lacking any economies of scale can break into market segments that were previously inaccessible due to the cost leadership advantages of large operators. Case Study 3 is a good example of how a small business has been created to meet the needs of an international market.

One of the biggest problems that befalls new websites is that their owner-operators fail to decide exactly what they want to achieve from them. The creation of a business website in its own right is an insufficient objective, particularly if it is intended to generate profit, or to contribute towards the development and growth of the business. When he was designing the website for wilderness-solutions.com, Doc Newman focused on the importance of formulating the key objectives of the website, and identified a number of specific questions to be answered:

- Why are you on the Web in the first place? Is it a question of personal enjoyment, ego, self-satisfaction, or are you seriously contemplating a profitable commercial venture?

- Who is your target or whom do you want your website to attract? This question is concerned with the demographic breakdown, activities, areas of common interest and motivating factors of your prospective audience. The important thing to remember is that the structure and combination of these will provide the determining factors in identifying the target audience and the appropriate external links (on your Internet site home page) needed to make contact with that audience. The target audience will also influence the content of your site, and the ways in which you advertise it.

- What do you want your site to do? What do you expect to accomplish on-line that cannot be accomplished else-

Pete (Doc) Newman has for many years been involved in climbing expeditions to remote parts of the world (Nepal, Patagonia, etc.), and during that time has climbed with a number of people who have become household names.

Although he is now a bit over the hill for climbing, he retains a strong interest in the subject. He had developed his expertise as the 'logistics' man for expeditions, i.e. the person who plans, organizes and assembles all of the necessary supplies and equipment for each expedition, getting these together in the right quantities, at the right place at the right time.

That is all very well in theory, but in practical terms, one of the major obstacles in this process is always the sourcing and acquisition of necessary specialist equipment, which with the restrictions of snail mail could take months of preliminary planning. In response to this situation, Pete and his colleagues decided to develop an Internet solution to the problem which would provide people such as themselves with a single-source solution to the problems of equipment acquisition and supply. This was an Internet site (www.wilderness-solutions.com, using the background image of Ayer's Rock) via which any prospective buyer could access the website to browse a wide range of specialist survival and expedition equipment, and could then order the required items knowing that they would be delivered to just about any reasonable location in the world (apart from the top of Everest) within seven days.

By virtue of existing trading relationships and contacts with major equipment suppliers, Pete was able to establish their agreement to distribute the equipment as and when ordered. Quite simply, a potential customer visits the website, selects one or more items, places an order and pays for the items via a secure credit card or payment system. After payment has been received, the order is sent to the supplier, who despatches the goods, after which the payment to the supplier for the goods is forwarded within seven days. The customers get rapid delivery of the goods they require from a single-source supplier, and that supplier gets rapid and secure payment plus a satisfactory profit margin as the net cost of the goods is transferred to them within a week, without incurring sales or credit costs of their own. Wilderness-solutions.com is able to make its own profit for promoting the goods and handling the transaction, and in short, everyone is happy. Once set up, the system requires little support or administration, save checking the monthly bank statements, suppliers' invoices and payments, etc. (I keep telling him, if only he didn't have so many ex-wives and mistresses strewn across the globe, he would be a millionaire by now!) Seriously though, it is a simple but brilliant idea that illustrates the opportunities that the Internet can offer small businesses to market their products on a worldwide basis.

where? For example, 'to increase annual sales by 10 per cent through on-line marketing'. The answer to this question entails the production of a list of specific objectives that you want to achieve with your Internet activities.

- On-line strategy decisions involve the process of reaching your target audience, e.g. should you use a commercial on-line service with its own established but broad audience, or should you use an ISP (Internet Service Provider) with which you might be able to target a more specific audience?

- The most obvious way to generate sales revenue is to provide a direct-response facility within your website, i.e. to provide a registration form, shopping basket and ordering service which they can immediately hook into once they enter the site. Apart from the fact that the shopping basket system acts as a sales tool in effectively asking the customer for the order, it also helps to stop them moving to another website to browse the offers there, and it enables special promotions to be linked to this service.

- Another key attraction of websites is the information and advisory services that they offer on a free-of-charge basis. People do not simply browse the Web for the sake of it – they are usually looking for something specific and useful, so make sure your website offers them just that. This is effectively the bait that may lead them actually to spend some money.

- Will you use Search Engine links, hyperlinks with other sites to increase your target audiences and to raise the profile of your business? Links can also be achieved (at much less cost) by contacting media sources and journalists associated with your particular industry, and this can be easily and cheaply achieved by sending them an e-mail inviting them to visit your site.

- If you have something to offer, then do not be afraid to show or demonstrate those items. Use pictures, diagrams, sound, video clips or interactive trials, but do not just describe them in text.

- The 'hits' you get on your website can provide invaluable market research information about both your products and services, and also the market in general. Do not be afraid to exploit this opportunity by using questionnaires or surveys to gain further information about your prospective customers.

- The website can also form a relatively inexpensive means of providing your customers with back-up service and support, in a format which can be much more convenient to you (and less exasperating to them) than on-line telephone services.

The three key words for website design, according to Doc Newman, are 'content, content and content'. This is what drives success on the Internet, attracts the punters, keeps their attention and makes them come back for more. A good Internet site will be easy to access, will enable fast recovery of pages (unlike so many UK university and government body sites) and will deliver up to date and relevant information in a timely and organized manner. He says: 'Obviously you will want to skew content towards your products and services. The trick is to do this in a way that doesn't appear self-serving. Make the content meaningful, relevant and ultimately helpful to your targets, and they will visit your site again and again. They'll even thank you for it.' Finally, decide who will be responsible and accountable for maintaining and updating the site and its content, and how often it will be updated. As Doc says: 'There is nothing more un-cool than a stale website!'

*Reference*

Paliwoda, S. J. and Thomas, M. J. (1998). *International Marketing*, 3rd Edn. Butterworth-Heinemann.

*Further reading*

*IM Business Checklists: Small Business Management* (1999). IM/ Hodder and Stoughton.
Webb, P. and Webb, S. (1999). *The Small Business Handbook*. Prentice Hall/FT.

# Chapter 7 Understanding
# Chapter 7 customers
# Chapter 7

Back in the mid-1980s, it was common to see in the reception areas of businesses a large poster depicting a magnificent male lion with the declaration beneath 'The Customer is King'. Many employees would also add to this the subscript that the customer can be a pain in the butt, but such often-deserved observations can only rightly be made out of earshot of those customers. However, the supplier–customer relationship has changed somewhat in recent years, with the customer no longer being viewed as a king who must be served and obeyed, but more as a long-term partner who shares a common interest with the business (however, that still does not stop some of them continuing to be a pain in the butt!).

This chapter is concerned with the issue of customer relations, and more specifically, with the understanding of customer perceptions as a critical factor in the development of future business strategy, with developing policies to meet those needs, and with creating an effective system of communications with customers. It matters little how brilliant an owner-manager is in devising long-term strategies for the business if those strategies are incompatible with the needs and perceptions of the customers, as the customers will simply buy elsewhere if they feel that the business is not meeting their needs. The chapter links to Units C1, C2, C3, C4 and D2 of the revised vocational standards.

## The import- ance of customer retention

In any business, there will inevitably be a turnover of customers, with a proportion dropping out each year and having to be replaced by new ones. In the case of retail customers for example, this natural wastage will normally occur as a result of changing customer needs or tastes, their purchasing power or residual income, their changing ages (e.g. children growing up, or workers retiring), or geographical movement. A less-natural wastage can also occur as a result of increased activity or aggressive pricing by competitors, or the company itself failing to give the customers the levels of quality and service they require.

For most small businesses, the sales force performs four main functions: servicing existing customers, persuading existing customers to purchase more, replacing customers lost through natural wastage, and obtaining new customers to expand the business. It is obvious, therefore, that if the firm can reduce the amount of time and effort expended by its sales force on replacing lost customers, then the time saved can be applied to both persuading existing customers to buy more, or to finding new customers to expand the business. The most obvious way to achieve this saving is by ensuring that the customers receive the standards of quality and levels of service which meet their needs and perceptions, thereby giving them no reason to take their business elsewhere. It is true that a percentage of customers will always buy on price alone irrespective of the service they receive. However, the vast majority of buyers are aware that, as well as being price conscious, it is equally important to consider other factors such as the quality of products or services, reliability and convenience of supply, product support and warranty facilities. These factors will inevitably have a cost to the supplier, but as the simple example in Case Study 4 illustrates, the potential returns can far outweigh the costs in the longer term.

Xavier Onassis runs a small business that imports and supplies Mediterranean foods to Greek and Italian restaurants. In recent years, he has had an average of 100 regular customers that generate between them sales revenue of £1 000 000 p.a. His overheads are £400 000 p.a., and his variable costs are 45 per cent of sales revenue. He loses an average of 20 per cent of his customers each year and employs two salesmen at a cost of £50 000 p.a. to replace these and to service existing customers. At the end of year 1 he decides that the business is going nowhere as his salesmen use all their spare time replacing lost custom. On investigation, he finds that reasons for losing such a high proportion of his customers are due to problems of reliability and poor service by his staff. He is advised to invest in staff training and to improve his operating and support systems for his customers. This will cost the equivalent of £300 per customer p.a., but will reduce his customer losses to 10 per cent p.a., allowing his sales staff to develop an extra 10 per cent of new business each year. The following table shows the impact of his decision:

**Case Study 4**

|  | Year 1 | Year 2 | Year 3 | Year 4 |
|---|---|---|---|---|
| Number of customers | 100 | 100 | 110 | 120 |
| Sales | 1 000 000 | 1 000 000 | 1 100 000 | 1 200 000 |
| Overheads | 400 000 | 400 000 | 400 000 | 400 000 |
| Variable costs | 450 000 | 450 000 | 495 000 | 540 000 |
| Sales costs | 50 000 | 50 000 | 50 000 | 50 000 |
| Customer care | 0 | 30 000 | 33 000 | 36 000 |
| Profit per customer | 1000 | 700 | 1220 | 1450 |
| Net profit | 100 000 | 70 000 | 122 000 | 174 000 |

This case study is a very simple example of how an investment in customer care, although it causes an initial drop in profits, can offer longer term benefits in the form of increased sales revenue, increased contribution per customer, and increased overall profits for the business. This is an example of the business maxim that 'quality costs nothing' in the long term, and customer care is, after all, an integral part of the quality policy for any business.

## Customer care

Customer service is often described as the way in which we respond to our customers and their problems, which implies an essential reactive process. In contrast, customer care takes a more proactive stance, more akin to a total quality management policy. The concept of customer care builds a policy of awareness and responsiveness to the customer within the provision of the product or service as a whole, and with the explicit intention of avoiding possible problems at a later stage. Customer care is about minimizing the occurrences that are likely to give rise to complaint, and responding quickly and positively when complaints do occur.

Customer care is concerned not just with the ways in which the needs of customers are identified and assessed, in terms of the products, goods and services that they require. It is concerned with the customers' expectations of the ways in which those products are provided, delivered and subsequently supported by the people involved in the organization. Customer care is about formulating and implementing policies and standards of behaviour and practice, which will ensure that customers needs are identified. It is also about developing procedures which ensure that customers are treated politely, fairly and positively if and when things go wrong, to ensure that customers are retained rather than lost. Invariably, the customer service policy will overlap with, and reflect, the sales and marketing plans, and the quality policy of the business, as it does in effect provide the mechanism by which the quality standards etc. are implemented within the sales and distribu-

107

tion environment. What must be remembered is that it is impossible to draw up an effective customer care policy without first identifying the factors that the customers themselves care about, i.e. what they expect from the contact they have with your business and the transactions they make with it.

The best way to appreciate the perceptions and expectations of people who have dealings with your business is to put yourself in their position. Imagine that you are calling on a business, unannounced, with the intention of finding out about their products or services, how they can be of use to you, what benefits they will offer, what they will cost, and how easily you can acquire them. Finally, imagine that you have your chequebook in your pocket, ready to place an immediate order if you can find the right deal. Okay, you arrive at the site, park outside (assuming you can get into the car park) and enter the premises. What do you expect to find?

**Customer perceptions and expectations**

- When you enter the premises you expect pleasant and suitable surroundings which are clean, welcoming, well-lit, safe and hygienic, and living up to the general image of the business and its products or services.

- At reception, you expect sufficient staff to be available, so that you are not kept waiting. You expect them to show a friendly, interested and welcoming attitude, to be pleasant, and most certainly non-threatening or aggressive. They should also be smart in appearance, competent and knowledgeable. You expect that your dealings with the organization's staff should be a pleasant experience, and free of problems, antagonism or excuses.

- From the products, goods or services, you would expect that these should be available when wanted, fit for the purpose for which they were acquired, and at a reasonable price which constitutes value for money. Information about the products should be provided as to where the product can be found, and its use and operation, and most important of all, that information should be user-friendly. The product should also be supported by a friendly, helpful and efficient after-sales service in the event of any problems arising, and the response to any problems should be both prompt and positive.

- When the products are delivered you expect them to be securely packaged, undamaged, the order should be complete and correct in every detail, and the associated paperwork should show the correct prices and discounts, the terms of trade, and should specify that payment is due on the date you have agreed with the vendor. Full information about warranties, or the actions to be taken in the event of problems, should be provided along with contact names and telephone numbers.

- In the event that a problem does arise, you expect to be able to contact someone promptly without being subjected to twenty minutes of agonizing Pan Pipes music interspersed by periodic shunting between the switchboard and various telephone extensions. You expect your problem to be dealt with promptly and politely, and that someone will offer you a quick and practical solution, with minimum inconvenience to you.

- Overall, you expect the whole process to be pleasant and painless, and you want to complete the transaction with the feeling that you have been treated as an important and valued customer. If you get that feeling you will not quibble too much about minor cost details; in fact, you will be likely to consider any extra cost to be more than justified by the high level of service you have received. Most important of all, you will want to come back for more!

Now just pause and think for a moment. Consider carefully: how does the above description compare with what your customers would find if they were to visit your premises unannounced? What changes do you need to make to bring your own business up to those standards, and how will you implement them? This is the starting point for formulating a customer care policy, but to make it work will require a very detailed scrutiny of all aspects of the business that interface with customers, or which might in some way have implications for the quality of service your customers receive. The Total Quality Management (TQM) concept is concerned with ensuring the highest possible quality of every single aspect of the operation of a business, including its staff, its management, its resources, its processes and its customers. Customer care is, in effect, the public face of TQM, and like TQM it should incorporate the concept of 'quality by design', building aspects of quality into the product or service provision right from the start in order to pre-empt and avoid potential problems at a later stage.

It is the prescribed standards of performance that form the backbone of any customer care policy, as unless the various processes of interaction with customers are measurable against defined standards, there is no way of telling whether or not the policies are working. The process then involves defining a comprehensive range of standards for each stage of the interaction with the customers, i.e. before, during and after the transactions, and then monitoring the achievement of those standards.

## *Quality standards for customer care*

Pre-transactional standards are concerned with the stage prior to the transaction, when contact with the customer is first established. These define the processes and responses required to keep the customer satisfied in the preliminary or enquiry stages of the sale. For example, a catering business providing wedding reception services might have for its pre-transactional standards:

- All enquiries will receive a telephone response within twenty-four hours.

- The owner will arrange an appointment with the clients within seven days to discuss their needs, and will provide sample menus, and photographs and references from previous functions.

- A written quotation will be posted to the client within forty-eight hours of the visit, giving a detailed schedule of the services to be provided, any options available and a firm estimate of costs for those items, and a summary of payment terms, etc. This will form the contract with the clients.

- On receipt of confirmation of the booking, a letter of acknowledgement will be sent to the clients requesting the agreed deposit or booking fee.

- Four weeks before the event, the client will be contacted to confirm any variations to the requirements, and an invoice will be raised for the balance.

- A week before the event, the client will be contacted again to finalize details of access arrangements, times and any special requirements, e.g. vegetarians, young children or wheelchair users.

- All necessary food and sundries will be ordered five days before the event for delivery on the day before the event, or early the same morning.

The transactional standards relate to the quality and provision of the actual transaction itself, the production and quality of goods or materials, the processes by which it will be delivered, and the standards that can be expected from the people involved. This is best illustrated using the same example of the catering business:

- All food items will be fresh, of high quality, and will be stored in suitable containers at safe temperatures prior to preparation and before they are served, in compliance with Environmental Health regulations.

- Food will be prepared as close as possible to the time of the event to ensure freshness and safety. It will be prepared in hygienic conditions, under the supervision of staff trained and qualified in food hygiene.

- Tables will be laid with clean cloths, crockery and cutlery, with decorations in the colours and designs prescribed by the customers.

- Waiting staff will be clean, tidy, polite and friendly. They will be dressed in a standard formal style appropriate to the event. Food will be served promptly and tables cleared quickly once the diners have finished eating.

Post-transactional standards are used to define levels of after-sales service, warranty conditions for products, locations of service centres, response or turnaround times, etc. They would also include how the service is completed and how feedback on service provision would be sought. Again, using the above example:

- After the meal all items will be cleared promptly, washed and removed from the site. Kitchen areas will be left in a clean and tidy condition, and all rubbish will be bagged for disposal.

- At the end of the event, the clients will be approached by the person in charge to check that there are no further requirements, and then thanked before departure.

- A week later the clients will be sent a letter enclosing a brief questionnaire and pre-paid envelope, requesting their feedback on the service provision.

The last of those post-transactional standards is particularly important, as there is little point in establishing a comprehensive list of standards and associated targets without some form of monitoring to ensure that they are being achieved. The feedback should be evaluated and used to modify the standards or to develop new standards.

**Customer communi-cations**

At the end of Chapter 4, we briefly mentioned the importance of establishing good working relationships with suppliers, and how these relationships should work both ways, each benefiting the other. Here the role has been reversed, and we have become the supplier rather than the customer, but the same type of relationships should apply. In the same way that our suppliers are looking to establish long-term stable supply relationships with ourselves, that is precisely what we want to achieve with our own customers, and the key to achieving this is regular contact and open exchange of information.

It is not sufficient to make a weekly telephone call to see if the customer wants to order anything, as that simply constitutes the bare minimum of effort to sustain whatever level of relationship that already does (or does not) exist. Building relationships with customers is about having regular face to face contact, talking to each other to establish points of common interest or mutual benefit, conducting open and honest negotiations, and developing an atmosphere of trust between the two organizations. Going back to the earlier part of this chapter, it is above all about listening to your customers (as opposed to just selling to them) and getting inside their heads to identify their expectations of your business and what it has to offer them. This does require a great deal of time and effort, but that is precisely why you employ sales staff. Any clerk can telephone a customer to take the details of an order, but the main skill that separates a top salesperson from an average one is their ability to establish and maintain relationships with customers. So, next time you tell the sales assistant to telephone Bloggs and Co. for their order this week, as you are too busy to call on them, just remember that one of your rivals might not be too busy to bother!

I am always amazed to hear how firms faced with financial pressures always make cutbacks in two key areas. The first is in training, which gives their staff the skills to provide the goods or services for the customers and to interface with them. The second is in sales, which generates the orders and long-term revenue that keeps the business going. The sales staff should form the primary link between customer and supplier, and one of their primary roles in talking to customers is to identify problem areas. Problems invite solutions, solving their problems generates sales income, and providing satisfactory solutions creates trust, boosts confidence and enhances your relationships with the customers. This is because the process of solving customers' problems gives the supplier an opportunity to exceed their customers' expectations. A customer who is impressed when their expectations are exceeded is one who will tell others of their experience, and the great benefit of this is that the customer starts to do your selling for you, and there is nothing like enthusiastic personal recommendation to promote your business!

The quality and customer care strategy must be based on a number of key factors: **Summary**

- A clear understanding of the needs, perceptions and expectations of the firm's customers.

- The establishment of clear standards of quality for customer transactions and support services.

- Careful design of the goods or services on offer to incorporate quality features or systems that will maximize their value to the customer, and minimize the risk of problems or failure.

- Well-defined lines of communication between the customers and their contact points in the business, and between the various parts of the business which form the supply chain to delivers the goods and services to the customer.

- Monitoring of the above factors to ensure that they are consistent, and that they contribute towards customer retention, to minimize customer losses, and to facilitate the full use of sales resources to be applied to growing current business and developing new business.

The customer care strategy itself must complement and work towards the overall long-term strategy of the business as a whole.

*Further reading*

Butler, D. (2000). *Business Planning: A Guide to Business Start-Up*, Chapter 11. Butterworth-Heinemann.

Canning, V. (1999). *Being Successful in Customer Care*. Blackhall.

Oakland, J. (1994). *Total Quality Management: The Route to Improving Performance*. Butterworth-Heinemann.

Rice, C. (1997). *Understanding Customers*. CIM/Butterworth-Heinemann.

Smith, I. (1997). *Meeting Customer Needs*. IM/Butterworth-Heinemann.

Stone, M. and Young, L. (1992). *Competitive Customer Care*. Croner.

# Chapter 8 Staffing the business

Chapter 8
Chapter 8

In a nutshell, Strategic Human Resources Management (known to lesser mortals as manpower planning) is all about getting the right people, with the right skills, in the right place, at the right time, and then providing the right structure and balance of motivation and reward to keep them there. This is hard enough to achieve in a large organization that has the resources to employ Human Resource Professionals (personnel managers), that can afford the necessary reward structures and opportunities for promotion or career development, and that can make use of highly specialized skills. However, as we have discussed a number of times in previous chapters, the average small firm does not have these luxuries, often lacking or possessing only limited resources, relying on the limited personnel knowledge of the boss and the willingness of the multi-skilled staff to be flexible in their work.

The revised vocational standards contain a number of Units relating to staff management; however, the majority of these are concerned with what are essentially operational issues. Unit J2 is about counselling, staff discipline and dismissal, Unit J3 relates to redeployment and redundancy (hardly an ideal objective for the owner-manager anticipating expansion), and Unit J4 is about recruitment and selection. Units K1, K3 and K4 are concerned with mentoring staff, and training and developing them to improve skills. This chapter will concentrate on Unit J1, that relates to the more strategic issues of auditing the existing staff resources, the numbers of staff and range of available skills etc., and the skills requirements of the business. Once the current resources have been mapped against the future needs of the business, and the gaps have been identified, it is then possible to develop a plan to fill those gaps in readiness for expansion. This will be achieved by training or promoting existing staff from within the organization, or by recruiting new experienced staff from outside, or by a combination of the two. Part of the process also involves the owner-managers themselves, as the skills gap analysis is not complete without an assessment of the management of the firm. This links with Units A3 and H1, which are concerned with the performance of the owner-managers and their organizational and time-planning abilities, and this is a very good place to start.

## Workforce planning

At a strategic level, this involves matching the skills of the key executives or managers to the needs of the strategic plan by identifying those management skills that are needed to achieve the long-term objectives of the business. For example, a policy of substantial growth that involves exporting as part of the process would normally require the business to have someone at policy-making level that possesses substantial skills and experience in international marketing. The strategic aspects would also involve the monitoring and appraisal of performance to ensure that (a) the managers are performing at a level that will enable the business to achieve its strategic targets, and (b) that skills are modified or developed on an ongoing basis in line with the changing needs of the business.

On a tactical level, manpower planning involves designing and creating a reward system that will provide and retain a stable and motivated workforce. It will involve anticipating future problems of surpluses or deficits of staff skills, possibly requiring the development of a more flexible workforce with a core of regular key staff supplemented by peripheral staff: temps, agency staff, part-time or seasonal workers. The tactical aspects are also concerned with medium-term staff development, career development, training plans, etc., as a means of reducing the dependence on external recruitment when skills are in short supply.

On an operational level, manpower planning is about the day-to-day recruitment and selection process, induction, staff training to facilitate immediate needs and to create multi-skilled staff to provide more flexibility, and to make the best (most productive) use of available human resources. It is also concerned with performance appraisal, administration, and the monitoring of reward structures and ongoing motivation.

**The owner-manager as a human resource**

The term 'owner-manager' is to the small business what 'entre-preneur' is to larger high-flying companies. It has probably been coined as a more appropriate alternative, as 'entrepreneur' has an almost flamboyant connotation which somehow does not quite match up to the small garage owner wearing a grease-covered boiler suit, working in a lock-up with rain leaking in through holes in the roof. Or perhaps 'owner-manager' just appeals to the English sense of understatement. In either case, whilst the 'owner' part of the label may be the case, the 'manager' part does not imply the automatic presence of any management skills, the title often being bestowed by virtue of position alone, rather than from knowledge or experience of managing a business. Just imagine if the French philosopher, Rene Descartes, had been an owner-manager, the whole meaning of life would have been transformed: '*Cogito ergo managum* – I manage therefore I am', and '*Sum res managans* – I am a managing thing'. Perhaps this is not so far away from the thinking of some managers after all!

As we have said before, when the business first starts up, the owner-manager must be all things to all men: the decision-maker, the salesman, the accountant, the buyer, the production manager, the debt collector, and often the labourer and toilet cleaner. As the business grows, specific roles can be allocated to other staff or specialist services can be bought in, e.g. the sales agent or the part-time book-keeper. However, no matter what specialist or technical skills the owner-manager can purchase or employ, there are three key skills which he or she must master: the ability to organize oneself, the ability to organize others and the ability to delegate. So, the questions:

- How well do I organize myself? Do I plan my time carefully to make full use of the working day, or do I flit from one job to another in response to calls or demands? Do I use a diary or planner to schedule regular activities, and allocate time around these for other work, or to respond to urgent items? Do I prioritize my work to take account of relative urgency and/or importance? Do I plan my travel efficiently to avoid wasted time or unnecessary distance?

- How well do I organize my staff and their work? Is the work planned in advance to meet customer orders or requirements, or do they always seem to be responding to 'emergencies'? Do I have a good working relationship with my staff? Do they think that I have a good relationship with them? Do they like or dislike me? Do I care about that? What style(s) of management do I use? Does my management style have a positive or neutral effect on them, or is it de-motivating? Can I handle staff problems or conflict comfortably? Do my staff feel that I am approachable?

- Do I delegate work effectively to others? Do I match the person to the task, or just give the job to the nearest one, or to my favourite? Do my staff welcome responsibility or shy away from it, and why is this so? Do I explain what I want them to achieve, how it is to be done, and what responsibility and authority they will have to complete the task? Do I provide the necessary training, support and resources to enable them to achieve the task? Do I keep in touch to monitor progress with new tasks? Do I give feedback and praise on their performance?

There are plenty of both long and short training courses to improve any of the above skills, but self-management and delegation skills are only really developed by practice, by doing them on a regular basis. Organizing and managing other people can be learnt from a book or a training course, but how effective that learning really becomes also depends on learning how to observe those people. By observing how they respond and react to your instructions or requests, by the verbal and non-verbal feedback they give, by watching their body language, by listening to what they tell you, and by monitoring their output or productivity.

When you buy a computer, a car, a van or a piece of production machinery, you or your accountant can perform some simple calculations to identify the outputs or benefits you will gain from the investment, how long it should last, the cost per annum over its lifetime, and the payback or return you will achieve on the investment. A delivery van might be good for five years, or a production machine for ten. Either way, you can be fairly sure that if you make the right choice in the first place, you will get a return on your investment. Unfortunately, people are not like that, and employing them can be both risky and expensive. So, you advertise for a skilled member of staff, you carry out a series of time-consuming interviews, select the person you want, and wait until they have worked their notice from current employment. When they start, you provide them with induction training, and perhaps product or job training, all this time running at less than optimum efficiency. Then three months later, just as your business is returning to full efficiency, they up and leave, and you have to go through the whole time-consuming and expensive process all over again. People are expensive to find, expensive to train, expensive to replace and inherently unreliable, that is unless you have the right motivation and reward structure to retain them.

Even if you do have the right structure in place, the on-costs of employing staff in terms of national insurance and pension

**The costs of employing staff**

contributions, sickness and maternity entitlements, annual holidays, cover for absence, training, uniforms or protective clothing, etc. can still add 30–40 per cent on top of the basic wage (and more if you run a business in parts of mainland Europe). The moral of all this is that it is imperative to make the right decisions about your recruitment and staff development policies, as mistakes can be very expensive.

## Symptoms of poor staff management or reward systems

The most obvious sign of a problem can be easily checked by measuring the annual rate of staff turnover within the business. There will always be some degree of natural staff turnover, e.g. resulting from retirement, staff moving to another area, health problems, or family commitments. The acceptable level of staff turnover will vary from one area to another, dependent on the stability of the local population, the supply of labour and the competing demands for that supply. In a rural area, where people tend to be less mobile and jobs less available, the percentage may be low, say 4 or 5 per cent. In an urban area, where there are more jobs around and the population is probably more mobile, 10 per cent may be nearer the norm. But, in either case, if the annual staff turnover (i.e. the percentage of leavers compared with the size of the total workforce) is above 15 or 20 per cent, then there is a clear problem. This may possibly be due to low levels of reward, or to poor working conditions, or unpleasant or repetitive work. On the other hand, the problem might also lie elsewhere, perhaps in the recruitment policy of the business, where the wrong type of staff are being recruited for the work, or inappropriate methods of selection are used.

Other symptoms of problems include rising rates of sickness or absenteeism, poor motivation resulting in reduced output, disruption of output, and most obviously, industrial action. It may well be the case that there is simply a shortage of suitably skilled workers in the geographical locality, in which case the firm must consider transporting them in from further afield, or introducing a training programme to develop them in-house.

121

| STAFF SKILLS AUDIT | SKILLS NEED AUDIT |
|---|---|
| • Matrix of current essential skills<br>• Evaluation of skills quality<br>• Spread of skills between staff<br>• Unused skills for future use | • Current skills needs<br>• Future requirements<br>• Quality and quantity<br>• Skills matrix/distribution<br>• Specialist skills needs |

**SKILLS GAP ANALYSIS**

• Comparison of needs and available skills
• Quality and quantity
• Identify gaps
• Job descriptions
• Person specifications
• 'Make or buy' decisions

| DEVELOP INTERNAL STAFF | EXTERNAL RECRUITMENT |
|---|---|
| • Internal promotion<br>• Training plans<br>• Mentoring and coaching<br>• NVQs/in-job training<br>• Formal training programmes<br>• Monitoring and evaluation | • Recruitment to replace natural wastage<br>• Recruitment to facilitate expansion<br>• Recruitment to facilitate changing skills requirements |

*Figure 8.1*   Skills gap analysis

This is often described as the 'grow-your-own or buy-in dilemma' (see Figure 8.1) arising from the skills gap analysis.

## Carrying out the skills audit

The first stage of this activity is concerned with identifying precisely what skills are needed, and the normal way of doing so is by drawing up a skills matrix. On one axis, you need to establish the jobs that are already occupied, and those which will be needed to accommodate growth or diversification. Remember that these must relate to the jobs themselves, and not the persons who occupy them. On the other axis are listed the range of skills needed for each of those jobs. Sources of information for this process include the job descriptions for the essential and desirable qualifications and experience needed for each post; if they do not exist, now is the time to remedy the situation. Standard Operating Procedures and product specifications can indicate the need for specific technical skills. Work or shift rotas can indicate gaps in secondary skills, such as first aid training, to ensure that there is normally a qualified first-aider on each shift. Minutes of meetings and reports can help to highlight deficiencies in skills that are causing problems for the business, and new product development information can point to future needs. Identifying those future needs is a particularly critical part of the process, as without having the right skills available in readiness for any planned expansion, the whole strategic plan for the business could be disrupted.

The second stage asks the question: who has the skills we need? It involves comparing the actual skills of those persons occupying the positions against the skills requirements of the jobs. The necessary information can normally be gathered from CVs and staff records, training records and appraisals, or by checking on previous qualifications and experience, courses attended, in-house training sessions completed, etc. If in doubt, you can always ask the supervisors or the staff themselves, and at the same time you can find out if they have any skills that you are not currently aware of, that might be useful in the future. It is always surprising how many people can offer useful transferable skills gained in previous jobs in the past.

| JOB ROLE | Ref. | Induction | Health and Safety | Manual Handling | OND Engineering | NVQ3 Supervisory Mgmt | NVQ2 Team Leader | F-T Driver course | Driving licence | First Aid Certificate | Assembly training | Packing and despatch | Customer service | Basic IT |
|---|---|---|---|---|---|---|---|---|---|---|---|---|---|---|
| **Production Department** | | | | | | | | | | | | | | |
| | | | | | | | | | | | | | | |
| **Assembler 1** | **A1** | # | # | # | | | # | | | # | # | | # | # |
| J. Jones | | Y | Y | Y | | | Y | | | Y | Y | | N | Y |
| **Assembler 2** | **A2** | # | # | # | | | | | | | # | | | |
| F. Smith | | Y | Y | Y | | | | | | | Y | | | |
| **Assembler 3** | **A3** | # | # | # | | | | | | | # | | | |
| J. Davies | | Y | Y | N | | | | | | | Y | | | |
| **Assembler 4** | **A4** | # | # | # | | | | | | | # | | | |
| R. Johnson | | Y | Y | N | | | | | | | Y | | | |
| **Assembler 5** | **A5** | # | # | # | | | | | | | # | | | |
| Vacant | | | | | | | | | | | | | | |
| **Assembler 6** | **A6** | # | # | # | | | | | | | | | | |
| Vacant | | | | | | | | | | | | | | |
| **Packer 1** | **P1** | # | # | # | | | | | | # | | # | # | |
| E. Elpus | | Y | Y | Y | | | | | | N | | Y | Y | |
| **Packer 2** | **P2** | # | # | # | | | | | | | | # | # | |
| D. Appy | | Y | Y | Y | | | | | | | | Y | Y | |
| **Maintenance Engr** | **Engr** | # | # | # | # | | | | | | | | | |
| A. Bodger | | Y | Y | Y | Y | | | | | | | | | |
| **Fork-lift driver** | **FD** | # | # | # | | | | # | # | | | | | |
| R. Ammer | | Y | Y | Y | | | | Y | Y | | | | | |
| **Supervisor** | **Sup** | # | # | # | # | # | | | | # | # | # | # | # |
| V. Bossy | | Y | Y | Y | Y | Y | | | | Y | Y | Y | N | Y |
| **Storeman** | **St** | # | # | # | | | | | | | | | # | # |
| S. Tackit | | Y | Y | | | | | | | | | | N | Y |
| **Van driver** | **Dr** | # | # | # | | | | # | # | | | # | # | |
| S. Peedy | | Y | Y | Y | | | | Y | Y | | | N | Y | |
| **Cleaner** | **Cl** | # | # | | | | | | | | | | | |
| M. Opup | | Y | Y | | | | | | | | | | | |
| | | | | | | | | | | | | | | |
| | | | | | | | | | | | | | | |
| # = skill needed | | | | | | | | | | | | | | |
| Y = training done | | | | | | | | | | | | | | |
| N = training needed | | | | | | | | | | | | | | |

*Figure 8.2*  Skills audit

The third stage involves matching the two against each other in order to highlight gaps between the ideal skills required adequately to perform each job role, and the actual skills that the occupants of those roles can demonstrate. This is what we mean by the skills gap analysis, i.e. what gaps have to be filled? The uncovered skills denote either areas for training and development or roles for which external recruitment will be needed to provide the essential skills. Some of the gaps may already have been picked up by the firm's appraisal process, if there is one in place. The two stages can be combined on a simple spreadsheet for each section or department of the business, as shown in the example in Figure 8.2.

## Lead time

The gap analysis should not just focus on current staff and existing vacancies. It should also be carried out for all employment needs in the foreseeable future. This will mean looking closely at the resources that have been identified as essential to meet the organization's strategic development, and what staff will be needed to operate or support those resources. Furthermore, it must examine the various stages of phases of growth, to ensure that the staff will be available in readiness for when they are needed. No business wants to have staff standing around idle, waiting for work to come in, but equally, no business can afford to be understaffed when that work does arrive. Irrespective of whether the staff are developed internally or recruited externally, there will inevitably be a lead time before they are fully operational, because both the training and development process and the recruitment and selection process can be extremely time-consuming.

## Grow your own or buy in?

The gaps that are identified by the matching process will form the basis for the development strategy of the business. That is, whether the business decides to plug the gaps by means of training and developing existing staff, or to recruit or buy-in ready-trained staff from the labour market. Recruiting staff who are ready-trained can be very attractive to a growing business. True, the advertising and selection process does cost time and money, but there can be equally significant savings elsewhere. For example, training costs can be high. Ready-trained staff provide an immediate saving on the cost and time required for training, and can quickly achieve a high level of efficiency or productivity in their jobs, whereas trainees may have to work up to that level over a period of time. It is also much more attractive from the owner-manager's perspective to buy-in ready trained staff rather than to train them yourself, raising their career expectations as you do so, and then seeing them move to a competitor a few months later. Is it not much better and cheaper, then, to poach the trained staff from your competitor in the first place? Perhaps, but it can also be short-sighted in that two or more firms competing for a limited number of skilled staff in a small locality can just end up creating a wages spiral for themselves.

We have said that internal promotion can take time and cost money; however, it also has its advantages, frequently in terms of the loyalty it can generate from promoted staff, who appreciate the promotion or development opportunities. Internal development also has the advantage of familiarity, in that existing staff are already comfortable with current systems within the business. The time needed to recruit externally can be particularly problematic if there is a fairly low level of local unemployment when local staff may be hard to find, or may cost above-average rates, or may have to be transported in from further afield. This is where internal development scores much higher than external recruitment. Equally, when there is a shortage of skilled labour in the locality, there simply may be no alternative other than to develop current staff, and then recruit less-skilled replacements to fill the gaps at the bottom.

In reality, the manpower planning strategy will not specifically choose to follow one or other option, but will select an appropriate combination of both, by selecting some staff for development and recruiting others from outside. The key factor

**The financial implications**

is to ensure that the chosen methods will enable the firm to get the right skills in the right place at the right time, to enable it to meet its strategic targets and objectives, whilst keeping costs down to an acceptable level.

As we have stated above, staff can be an extremely expensive but notoriously unreliable resource of the business. Once the staffing levels and skills requirements have been identified, the costs of these need to be fed into the financial plan for the business. As we mentioned above when considering the costs of employing staff, those costs do not just relate to the basic salary or wages. The on-costs of National Insurance, pensions, uniforms, annual leave, cover for sickness, absence or maternity leave, etc. can easily add another 30 per cent to the annual bill for each member of staff. There is also the added cost of administering the payroll systems, tax credits, stakeholder pensions, etc., which small firms are now obliged to provide and administer. Advertising costs, staff time for sifting applications and interviewing potential candidates all have a cost, particularly if the owner-manager is having to forego potential sales activities to attend interviews. Recruitment agencies can reduce that time commitment, but they themselves may charge up to 20 per cent of the first year's salary as their commission. Pre-expansion training for current staff and induction training for new staff will also add to the costs. So, when preparing the budgetary and cash-flow forecasts for expansion programmes, it is essential to build an allocation within the budget for these indirect costs, many of which will be incurred up front. It is easy to see why many modern businesses, particularly those involved in manufacturing, prefer to use robotic systems – and they do not answer back, or throw a sickie on a busy Monday morning, and you never hear of a robot claiming sexual harassment in the office!

Good selection and carefully planned staff development policies are an essential prerequisite for efficient business performance, but are still ineffective unless backed up by carefully designed reward systems. This is where many organizations go wrong, by putting the recruitment and training in place, only to cut corners by offering minimal wages or very basic other benefits, and then experiencing enormous levels of staff turnover, which push their operating costs through the roof. The reward system is the final link in the chain. Rates of pay and other conditions of employment must be sufficient to attract staff, to retain them and to motivate them to willingly contribute to meeting the objectives of the organization. The system must be capable of influencing the internal culture of the business, to encourage initiative and innovation, and it must reward responsibility within the structure of the business.

There is no golden rule or formula to get this right, as the optimum system will depend on the nature of the business. Job-based pay with annual reviews, if set at the right levels, can encourage loyalty and stability in the workforce, but motivation and performance may be enhanced by team bonuses or profit share systems. Individual bonuses or performance-related pay is highly motivating for individuals and encourages initiative, but can be a nightmare to administer when all staff are on different rates. Performance-related pay can have a negative effect on less able staff, and can often encourage competition rather than co-operation between staff. Financial reward can also be of particular significance to staff of small firms where there may not be any opportunities for advancement due to the small size of the firm.

It is particularly important for the owner-manager to keep a weather-eye on local wage rates and the supply and demand for skilled labour in the area. If these rates are high due to relatively low levels of local unemployment, then cost-cutting exercises to save on wages costs will only be counter-productive, and will result in staff leaving for better pay elsewhere. This goes back to what was said earlier about staff turnover levels, with the costs of replacing staff outstripping the marginal extra cost of retaining them in the first place, but more important than the cost is the disruption it can cause in achieving the strategic objectives. In summary then, the reward structure is the key to successful manpower planning, and getting it right is just as important to the business as the recruitment, retention and development of staff.

As a footnote to this chapter, back in Chapter 1 (the political context) it was mentioned that, for the past twenty years or so, government has finally recognized the importance of small firms as the major source of employment opportunities for the future. In consequence, successive governments have introduced a range of support services to assist and encourage SMEs to help them reduce the impact of politically embarrassing unemployment statistics. Smallbone and Wyer (2000) argue that 'one of the issues that needs to be recognized in any discussion of small business growth is that not all owners see growth as an important business objective'. They argue that 'although employment generation may be an appropriate growth criterion for public policy, for most SME owners and managers it is a consequence rather than an important business objective'. This is an interesting and very true observation. The fact is that growth in the small firms sector is frequently driven by the objective of increasing the owner-managers' personal profits, as opposed to the view of many large organizations that growth should be an objective in its own right. The growth of employment potential as the business expands is very much incidental, and is rarely seen to be of major consequence to the strategic objectives of the average owner-manager, who most certainly does not see him or her self as the key facilitator of government employment policy.

Furthermore, the heavy burden of red tape imposed by government on all employers in recent years has fallen disproportionately on smaller firms. This has resulted in the inevitable attitude from owner-managers that employing extra staff is just a necessary evil that must be accepted when they need those extra staff in order to grow their businesses. As long as successive governments continue to nurture the vision of small firms as the major source of employment, presumably the small business support organizations will endure. However, one wonders what would happen if the Whitehall mandarins suddenly woke up to the fact that whether or not employment continues to grow in the small firms sector is not so much a consequence of their intervention and support policies, as the personal objectives and individual actions of some 3.7 million owner-managers, many of whom would gladly stick their fingers up to Whitehall at the first opportunity. Could it be that the concept of employees as an expensive and unreliable resource obviously does not ring any bells amongst Whitehall mandarins, or is it just that they have never tried to run a small business?

## References

Smallbone, D. and Wyer, P. (2000). In *Enterprise and Small Business, Principles, Practice and Policy* (S. Carter and D. Jones-Evans, eds), Chapter 23. FT/Prentice Hall.

## Further reading

Armstrong, M. (1995). *A Handbook of Personnel Management Practice*. Kogan Page.

Butler, D. (2000). *Business Planning: A Guide to Business Start-Up*, Chapter 4. Butterworth-Heinemann.

Gibbons, B. (1999). *If You Want to Make God Really Laugh, Show Him Your Business Plan*. Capstone.

Lasher, W. (1999). *Strategic Thinking in Smaller Businesses and Divisions*. Blackwell.

Thomson, R. and Mabey, C. (1994). *Developing Human Resources*. Butterworth-Heinemann.

# Chapter 9 Evaluating
# Chapter 9 financial
# Chapter 9 performance

In the same way that in the foregoing chapters we have examined and systematically evaluated the performance of the business in relation to its operating environments, its resource requirements, its sales and marketing performance, its managerial capabilities, and its staff management, we now have to look more closely at the financial performance to date, and the financial systems the business currently employs. In terms of the revised vocational standards, this process relates to Units A2, G1 and G4.

If anything, financial performance has got to be one of the easier areas to evaluate, because it is measured against what is essentially factual information, but in practice this is not simply a case of just comparing the factual data on a year-on-year basis. Such comparisons only tell the analyst about what is happening within the organization over a period of time, and not what is happening in a wider context, i.e. how the business is performing in the market environment, and how it is performing in the light of changes in that market. Achievement cannot just be assessed by actual performance alone, it has to be assessed in relation to the market environment in which the organization operates. For example, a business that has sales of £1 million in a market worth £10 million in 2001 has a 10 per cent share of the market. However, if in 2002 the sales increase by 10 per cent to £1.1 million, but the overall market size grows by 20 per cent to £12 million, then although the company's sales have grown significantly, its overall market share has decreased from 10 to 9.17 per cent, as rival businesses must have gained a greater market share during the year.

In the 1990s, there was a popular move towards benchmarking as a means of evaluating organizational performance, particularly in the public sector. The benchmarking process aims to assess the relative efficiency of service provision, particularly in public sector organizations (where profit is rarely regarded as a relevant performance indicator, and for that matter, neither is break-even), by comparing their achievements with other organizations of a similar type and size, that provide the same or similar services. The key to the comparisons lies in first identifying areas of 'best practice' against which the performance of others can be matched, based on the principle that no one organization has the monopoly on best practice. Whilst this process may be fine with the relatively well-resourced larger public sector bodies, such as local councils and health authorities (although they would probably refute that they are well resourced, even compared with small firms), in the small firms context benchmarking is a less attractive and less practical option. Similarly, larger private sector organizations are able to 'benchmark' themselves against the performance of their rivals, perhaps by comparing the data in published annual accounts, or against market research data for specific industrial or service sectors. Other sources of comparative data might include government-published statistics, trade or professional journals, business journals (e.g. *The Economist*, or *Fortune* in the USA).

Benchmarking is also employable in the private sector, and not just for service industries, although the emphasis is on comparison with the performance levels of other similar organizations rather than comparison with best practice. After all, best practice in competitive commercial terms is all about optimizing performance to maximize profit. ICL is said to benchmark itself against twenty rivals in the computer industry on four main points: the ratios of average debtors and creditors to sales turnover, the spending on research and development compared with sales turnover, the return on capital invested, and the sales revenue per head of employees (personally, I think that makes five). When it comes to benchmarking the average small firm hits three major obstacles. First, it rarely has the resources to devote to surveying and analysis the data. Second, as most of the data are collated from information relating to big companies, its relevance to the small firm is questionable, or at the very least, hard to accurately evaluate. Can a small PC assembly company or a local software sales and support business gain any genuinely applicable market intelligence by benchmarking itself against a long-established international player and its twenty major rivals? Thirdly, there is still relatively little comparative performance data about small firms in specific industries, although that situation is slowly improving.

## Accounting ratios

Given the inherent shortfalls of benchmarking in the small firms sector, the standard and established alternative method of evaluating financial performance lies in the use of accounting ratios. These compare facts and figures gleaned from the annual accounts of businesses, and provide year-on-year data about performance in key areas for comparison. However, as stated above, these data are essentially concerned with internal performance, and do not make comparisons with the overall market environment, although they do facilitate year-on-year comparison. Accounting ratios are primarily tools that can be used to assess the performance of the business, particularly in terms of solvency and liquidity. There is a range of ratios that can be applied to test different aspects of business performance, but we will just concentrate on some of those that are of significance to the small business.

### Liquidity ratios

- The Working Capital ratio (also called the Current ratio) tests the short-term liquidity of a business. It compares the current assets (cash, stock, debtors, work in progress) to the current liabilities (bills falling due for payment). Ideally, the current assets : current liability ratio should be 2:1. If the ratio is less, then stock levels or credit facilities given to customers may be too high.

- The Liquidity ratio (also called the Acid test or Quick ratio) is a more precise measure of liquidity, as it compares the liquid assets of the business (current assets less slow-moving stock or bad debts) with the current liabilities. The liquid assets when compared to current liabilities should show a ratio of at least 1:1 to demonstrate that the business can meet its current obligations, i.e. it can pay its creditors on time.

- The other way to check on solvency is to compare the average credit given with the average credit taken. In the first case we take the average outstanding debtors figure × 365, divided by the sales turnover. For example, an average outstanding debt of £20 000 compared with an annual turnover of £240 000 is one-twelfth of 365 days, which equals approximately 30 days. An average credit taken of £24 000 compared with the same turnover equals one-tenth of 365 days, i.e. 36.5 days. It is obviously more advantageous for the cash flow and working capital of the business to give 30 days' credit to customers, and to take 36.5 days' credit from suppliers.

## Borrowing capacity

- The Gearing ratio is more concerned with solvency, as it compares the equity (or share capital) and reserves of the business with its long-term liabilities (loans, mortgages and preference shares), to ensure that loans etc. can be repaid if the business should cease trading. In simple terms, it compares the resources supplied by the owners with the resources borrowed from others, to ensure that the first exceeds the second. The preference shares are lumped in with the long-term liabilities simply because the dividends on these have to be paid before any ordinary share dividends can be considered. This ratio is regarded as a good measure of the borrowing capacity of the business, as the higher the ratio, the better the borrowing potential.

- The Asset Cover ratio compares total assets with total debt to determine how many times the debts of the business are covered by its assets. This again reflects the borrowing capacity of the business, as the higher the ratio, the more it is likely to be able to borrow, because it is seen to have the surplus resources to cover further debt. The borrowing capacity is of interest not just to providers of long-term liability funds (bankers, debenture and mortgage lenders, etc.) but to the 'current liabilities', the ordinary suppliers and creditors who want to be assured that their credit is adequately covered by assets.

- The Net Asset Value compares the ordinary shareholders' funds (capital and reserves, etc.) with the number of shares issued. This measures the value of the assets of the business that are attributable to each share. So, a business with assets worth £4.00 for each £1.00 share issued would generally be regarded by a lender as being a better risk than one with assets worth just £1.50 per £1.00 share.

## Profitability ratios

- The Return on Capital Employed (ROCE) compares the profit received from ordinary trading activities before interest, with the sum of the capital employed in trading. It is expressed as a percentage. For example, if the company employs capital of £100 000 and produces a profit from ordinary trading of £30 000, it has made a Return on Capital Employed of 30 per cent. This ratio is of key interest to potential investors. It is also important to remember that if the ratio falls below the average level of interest paid on bank deposits or investments, then the business would be better off not trading, and just leaving its capital on deposit at the bank. In the case of owner-managers, this means that they would be better off shoving their money in the building society or some other form of investment, and getting a job working for someone else. The reduction in stress would probably also increase their life expectancy in the process! The point of this is that if you are working for yourself, you should expect a reasonable return on the time, money and energy you expend in running the business, and that the level of return should be demonstrably greater than that which could be achieved by leaving your money in the bank, and working for someone else (job satisfaction aside). The ROCE provides the means of comparing your results with the softer option.

- The Earnings per share ratio compares the net profit after tax, less preference share dividends, with the number of ordinary shares issued. In very simple terms, the amount of tax paid profit that could possibly be distributed amongst shareholders, divided by the number of shares eligible to receive it.

- Gross profit compared to turnover is another good indicator of profitability, especially on a year-on-year basis, as is also the operating profit to turnover ratio (gross profit less distribution and administration costs divided by sales turnover). However, these do not always necessarily correspond with each other year-on-year, if changes have occurred in distribution and administration costs during the year.

- Another measure of profitability is the comparison between sales turnover and the number of employees in the organization, usually expressed in terms of thousands of pounds per head. Variants include comparisons of operating profit to turnover and net fixed assets to turnover. These ratios tend to be more popular in the USA than the UK, and can influence stock exchange values on the

US stock markets. Whilst not particularly relevant to the small firms sector, these comparisons do actually influence the employment policies of large multinationals. Pfizer Pharmaceuticals, for example, employ large numbers of permanent contract staff in their UK locations for security and administrative duties, in order to maintain the ratio to their advantage in overseas stock markets. Those contract staff simply appear as an expense item on the profit and loss account. There is, of course, nothing illegal or improper about this practice, and it creates a lot of opportunities for the smaller local contract companies that supply the staff. However, employment policies such as these might create a false impression amongst individual US investors who had not taken the trouble to familiarize themselves with the details of the policies, or any relevant disclosures in the published accounts.

## Efficiency ratios

- There are quite a few of these to choose from; for example, the working capital (current assets less current liabilities) to sales turnover ratio tests the number of times the working capital is being utilized each year. This is a measure of how well the business is using its resources, although obviously what is deemed as a satisfactory or good ratio will depend on the market in which the business operates. A wholesaler or retailer of foodstuffs will turn over its stock rapidly, so in turn the working capital will have been used on a regular basis, perhaps weekly. In contrast, a manufacturer of specialist engineering machinery, that could take six months to build, install and commission, may only turn over its working capital a few times each year. This is the contrast between a low-profit/high-turnover business and a high-profit/low-turnover business.

- The same comparison can be made using the whole capital employed by the business in relation to sales turnover to determine how frequently that is being utilized, but again, the outcomes must be reviewed in the context of what is satisfactory or good for the market in which the business operates.

- By comparing the ratio of the average stock held against the total value of stock purchased in the course of the trading year, it is possible to determine how fast and how efficiently the stock is being turned over. For example, an average stock of £10 000 compared with a total annual purchase of £730 000 over 365 days would indicate that the stock is being turned over, i.e. sold, every five days. This figure in itself is not particularly helpful unless compared or benchmarked in some way with an industrial average. For example, a branch of Sainsbury or Tesco supermarkets might expect to turn their stock of baked beans over every couple of days, and their bread almost daily, but a furniture retailer, such as Courts, would no doubt be more than happy to turn all of their stock over once each month.

- It is also possible to evaluate a whole range of specific costs as a percentage of sales turnover, for example sales costs, marketing costs, production costs, distribution costs, administration costs, etc., in the same way. In their own right, these are not necessarily immediately useful, but when compared year-on-year they can be a good indicator of changing patterns of performance within the business. For example, they may highlight how one cost area might be rising disproportionately in comparison with others, or perhaps to explain why the ratios of gross profit to turnover, and operating profit to turnover, may not be moving in the same direction or at the same rate, as mentioned earlier.

# Cash management

The key to the survival of any business is cash flow, because if cash does not flow into the business at an adequate rate to maintain the level of working capital, then the business will struggle to survive. The working capital is defined in terms of current or short-term assets (petty cash, cash in the current account, stock, work in progress, and cash owed to the business) minus the current liabilities (overdrafts, money owed to suppliers or other creditors, etc.). If there is not a positive difference between the two, then the business cannot pay its bills on time. If cash flow is poorly managed or if the rate of expansion outstrips the size of the working capital (a situation known as over-trading), then only the goodwill of the banks and the creditors will keep the business going. In reality, neither of those groups can afford to be philanthropic when faced with repeated late payments, which are a sure sign of a potential risk; well, perhaps a little philanthropy from the banking sector would not go amiss at times.

Any business that is planning to diversify or grow must first ensure that it has adequate working capital in place to facilitate the expansion, and second, that it has suitable systems in place to monitor and control its cash flow. Unless the business operates in a strictly cash environment, any expansion will require the giving of a higher volume of credit than is currently the case. Whilst corresponding increased credit can usually be obtained from its suppliers, there will always be a gap between the two, i.e. the cost of the added value, and the profit margin which the business must make. It is the added value part, the staff wages, the overhead costs, distribution expenses, etc., that the working capital must bridge until the goods or services are paid for, and the more that is sold, the more the funds that are needed to bridge the gap. Without the working capital to bridge this gap, the firm will end up over-trading, which apart from being illegal (in that it is trading insolvently because it cannot pay its creditors when due) is a straightforward recipe for disaster. Many highly profitable firms have gone under because they have attempted to expand faster than their working capital would allow, and have simply run out of money with which to operate the business on a day-to-day basis.

- The net profit from trading (assuming of course that all debtors pay on time). As trading profits increase, they will increase the amount of working capital available, but equally, any losses will diminish working capital.

- The sale of fixed assets will increase the cash available to run the business, but any corresponding or subsequent purchase of fixed assets will reduce that sum. When a vehicle is sold at the end of its practical working life, the residual value will be added to the working capital pot. However, any replacement vehicle (which will inevitably cost more on account of inflation over the intervening years) will probably result in a larger sum being taken out of the working capital pot, unless other financial provisions are made.

- When a long-term loan is taken out (or any other long-term liability), the working capital pot is increased; however, any regular repayments of loan capital and interest will progressively diminish the available balance.

- Injections of extra share capital will also increase the available working capital, but this receipt will again be counter-balanced by the payment of dividends to shareholders and the taxation of profits.

- Receipts from investments (interest or dividends) will add to the pot, but these are also liable to taxation.

- Changes in the average balance of debtors and creditors are major influences on the available working capital. Increased creditors (more credit from suppliers) and decreased debtors (faster payment by customers) will both improve the cash flow, whilst conversely, the reduction in creditors and any increase in debtors will worsen cash flow. The latter is one of the inevitable effects of any growth in trading.

- Increased stockholding, which may be necessary in response to growth in demand, will reduce the amounts of cash available, but if stocks can be reduced, e.g. by

*Main factors that influence cash flow*

switching to just-in-time deliveries by suppliers or by simply reducing the average levels of stocks held, then cash can be freed for other purposes.

Each one of the above aspects needs a definitive policy and careful management if the available working capital is to be optimized, because it is easy for any one of them to get out of control and to wreck the effects of careful cash management in the other areas. For example, the benefits of a tight credit control policy can easily be wiped out by the loss of available spare cash due to overstocking or by not making best use of available credit from suppliers.

## Credit management

How can we develop an effective credit control policy that will make a positive contribution to the business? The first objective must be to ensure the correct balance of debtors and creditors, i.e. that the overall level of credit given to customers does not exceed the overall level of credit received from suppliers. As described earlier, this is easily checked by comparing the average debtor-days with the average creditor-days. However, that comparison alone will not suffice. Consider the situation where we take an average of £50 000 of credit on an average of £100 000 of purchases per month, resulting in a figure of fifteen creditor-days. At the same time, we give our customers an average of £60 000 of credit on sales of £150 000 per month, which works out at twelve debtor-days. On the face of things, this looks good in that we are giving twelve days' credit but receiving fifteen days' credit. However, in reality, we are giving an average of £60 000 credit each month but only receiving £50 000, which causes a net outflow of working capital. In a situation where the business is seeking a rapid expansion of trade, this is likely to be a common occurrence, and the actual cash figures should not be ignored just because the ratios look to be acceptable.

Getting the right balance involves ensuring that both the periods of credit and the total sums involved are both in our favour.

141

The above imbalance might be addressed by offering prompt payment incentives to reduce the debtors' figure. Alternatively, we could negotiate with our own creditors for longer payment terms, so that the average outstanding payments owed to them were larger that the debtors figure, say sixty-day payment terms rather than thirty-day. If the business is growing, the trade-off incentive to the suppliers might be the opportunity to deliver larger consignments of goods in one drop, requesting improved credit terms as an alternative to bulk quantity discounts. Remember there has got to be something in the deal to make it worthwhile to the supplier.

Another factor to bear in mind is that when trying to establish a balance between the overall debtors and creditors, it is not necessary for every single one of them to be in balance. For example, there may be one or two highly valued customers with whom you have negotiated special terms, e.g. extended credit for larger orders or long-term contracts. These could easily be counter-balanced by other customers to whom you give discounts for cash on delivery, or other prompt payment terms, such as within seven or fourteen days of invoice. It is the overall balance that is important to achieve.

In any period of expansion, it is also important to have a clearly defined credit control policy. Without going into great detail about credit control activity and debt collection techniques (these are outlined in Butler, 2000, pp. 133–7), it is necessary for the sales or accounts staff (or whoever deals with outstanding debts) to have clear guidelines to follow. These might include:

- Specified credit limits for each customer, which they cannot exceed without either payment or the owner-manager's specific authority.

- Specified dates or points at which the various credit control activities are triggered, for example initial reminder telephone calls, reminder letters, warning letters, supplies stopped, legal action commenced, etc. Once established, these should be adhered to firmly. Simply monitoring the aged debtors analysis generated by the accounting system at the end of each month is insufficient, there needs to be a designated person in the business who has the specific responsibility of monitoring payments due, on a daily basis.

- Clearly defined responsibilities for debt recovery and customer liaison. There is nothing worse than one person in the business chasing a customer for late payment, whilst the salesman is on the premises trying to get further orders. This happens frequently, and particularly in smaller firms where the financial and customer information systems are less likely to be fully integrated.

- Good working systems to ensure that the creditors of the business are paid on time, to ensure the maintenance of the supply chain, and to avoid the embarrassment of unavailable stock when your supplier will not deliver until your cheque is cleared.

- A contingency plan in case of emergencies, e.g. seasonal disruption of trade through bad weather. This is where the budgetary plan and cash flow forecast can help identify potential problems, and where, for example, temporary overdraft facilities can be arranged well in advance in readiness for any problems. Apart from the arrangement fee, an overdraft only incurs charges if and when it is used, although the fact that it is available should not tempt you to use it unless it is really required.

## Budgetary planning and cash flow forecasting

I am assuming that any owner-manager readers who are contemplating the expansion of their business will have previously prepared at least one budgetary plan to satisfy a potential bank manager, and will therefore be fully familiar with the grief this process can cause us lesser mortals who do not aspire to the lofty elevations of qualified accountants. In the early stages of a new business, it is very easy to overlook, or at least to underestimate, the importance of the budgetary planning process. Quite often, owner-managers will simply use broad estimates for input data, or will just focus on major items of income or expenditure, failing fully to consider the detailed costs involved. At the outset this may be due to lack of awareness of all of the cost factors involved in running a business, but as the firm grows it may also be due to a lack of attention to detail, or possibly a lack of the appropriate skills needed to evaluate the full cost implications of running the business. However, once the owner-manager is faced with making strategic decisions about the long-term future of the firm, the finer details can no longer be ignored, and every single aspect of income and expenditure must be considered in detail and incorporated into the budgetary plan. Once it has been established, we can start the really important part, that of identifying how the budget will be influenced and will need adjustment to accommodate cash factors:

- Cash balances brought forward from the previous period.

- Payments due to suppliers (creditors) incurred in the previous period.

- Payments due from customers (debtors) owing from the previous period, and adjustments for bad debts.

- Ongoing credit being given and received during the year.

- Receipts of loan income or capital.

- Purchase or disposal of fixed assets, lease payments, loan repayments, etc.

- In the case of sole traders and partnerships, the income tax liability for the business in the previous year, and with limited companies, the corporation tax liability for the previous period.

Faced with a period of expansion or diversification, there will inevitably be a number of abnormal pressures on cash flow, initially in the form of extra expenses incurred by the expan-

**SUMMARY BUDGETARY PLAN XYZ TRADING LTD**

|  | Month 1 £ | Month 2 £ | Month 3 £ | Month 4 £ |
|---|---|---|---|---|
| Sales income: | 150 000 | 160 000 | 170 000 | 170 000 |
| Expenditure: |  |  |  |  |
| Overheads | 40 000 | 40 000 | 40 000 | 150 000 |
| Stock purchases | 75 000 | 80 000 | 85 000 | 150 000 |
| Operating costs | 30 000 | 32 000 | 34 000 | 150 000 |
| Net inc. /exp. | 5000 | 8000 | 11 000 | 11 000 |

Assume:
– The previous two month's figures sales were £140 000, purchases were £70 000.
– 60 days' credit is given on goods sold.
– 30 days' credit is received on purchases.
– Operating costs and overheads are paid in the months in which they are incurred.

**SUMMARY CASH FLOW FORECAST XYZ TRADING LTD**

|  | Month 1 £ | Month 2 £ | Month 3 £ | Month 4 £ |
|---|---|---|---|---|
| Sales income: | 140 000 | 140 000 | 150 000 | 160 000 |
| Expenditure: |  |  |  |  |
| Overheads | 40 000 | 40 000 | 40 000 | 40 000 |
| Stock purchases | 70 000 | 75 000 | 80 000 | 85 000 |
| Operating costs | 30 000 | 32 000 | 34 000 | 34 000 |
| Net inc. /exp. | Nil | –7000 | –4000 | 1000 |

**DIFFERENCE BETWEEN BUDGET FIGURES AND CASH BALANCES**

| Month 1 £ | Month 2 £ | Month 3 £ | Month 4 £ |
|---|---|---|---|
| –5000 | –15 000 | –15 000 | –10 000 |

Note how the deficit increases as the monthly sales figures rise, and the huge drain on cash reserves, in spite of profitability.

*Figure 9.1* Budget and cash flow comparison

sion, but subsequently by the credit gap that can be the result of increased sales and credit given to customers. An example of the credit gap, and the difference between budget plan figures and cash flow forecast figures, is shown in Figure 9.1. This illustrates the negative cash flow resulting from a combination of increased sales and an imbalance of credit received and credit given, in spite of profitability. The sums involved would be hard to sustain over a period of time without substantial working capital, and the interest charges incurred in borrowing to bridge the gap would considerably reduce the profit margin.

I never cease to be amazed at the number of small business owners who are obliged to prepare an annual budget and cash flow forecast for their bank manager, and yet who shove it in the filing cabinet drawer and forget it until next year, once the bank manager has approved it. The budgetary process in any business should be a constant cycle of plan, implement, monitor and review. You plan the budget, start trading, monitor the actual income and expenditure by comparing it with the forecasts (at frequent and regular intervals), and review it to identify any problems and their causes and potential remedies. Every owner-manager knows that accounts and paperwork are an administrative pain in the neck, but the monitoring of budgeted figures against actual outcomes is the most critical pain in the neck of all, and if ignored, can turn into a terminal problem for the business.

*Financial monitoring and budgetary control*

Once again, the importance of an efficient budgetary control system comes to the fore when the firm is faced with expansion or diversification, because the budget monitoring system should form the yardstick for monitoring the effectiveness of the expansion. The monthly comparison actual versus forecast income and expenditure will give feedback on a number of key performance indicators against which the strategic plans for expansion can be measured. There are also a number of questions that must be asked in response to any variances in the outcomes:

- Are the actual levels of sales revenue in line with the fore-casts? Are there any fluctuations and can these be explained to our satisfaction? If not, what has happened and how do we respond to the fluctuations?

- Are there any unforeseen longer-term changes or trends in the pattern of demand? What are the causes? How should we respond to these? Do we have the capacity to respond to them?

- Are the profitability and cash flow figures acceptable? If not, where are the variances, and what are the reasons for these? What action do we need to take?

- Are the changing costs of overheads, raw materials, labour, sales and marketing, transport and distribution, adminis-tration, etc. acceptable or do we need to look closely at specific items? What will be the impact of these changes on our profitability? Should we be considering changes to our mark-up or selling prices?

- Are our sales activities and advertising campaigns work-ing? Are they having a positive effect on sales? If not, why not? Are we doing anything wrong? Are we missing something? What else should we be doing?

- Is our current working capital sufficient for our future requirements, or are we likely to hit cash flow problems? How soon will these problems occur? Do we have suffi-cient reserves, or do we need to arrange additional finance? Is the problem temporary, requiring a short-term over-draft, or do we need longer-term finance to increase available working capital?

- Will any current or likely changes in interest rates and exchange rates affect our operating costs or profit (partic-ularly if we are exporting our goods or services)? What action do we need to take to minimize the effects of this?

Monitoring the budgetary plans and the actual cash flow of the business is the most important process in assuring that

147

strategic objectives are being achieved. Quite simply, the budgetary comparison will tell you whether or not you are making a profit on an ongoing basis, and should enable you to highlight any problem areas if you ask yourself the right questions. Monitoring the cash flow situation will tell you if you are sufficiently solvent to continue trading, and if controlled closely, will alert you to potential problems. In this respect, whilst monitoring of actual against budgeted expenditure can be carried out monthly, cash flow monitoring does need to be carried out on a weekly basis, and in times of difficulty, on a daily basis.

*Reference*

Butler, D. (2000). *Business Planning: A Guide to Business Start-Up.* Butterworth-Heinemann.

# Chapter 10 Planning
# Chapter 10 financial
# Chapter 10 requirements

This chapter is concerned with forecasting the costs of implementing the strategic objectives, and ensuring that sufficient funding is available to enable them to be implemented efficiently and effectively. It will also look at the sources of finance available to expanding businesses. The chapter relates to Units G1, G2 and G3 of the revised vocational standards for Business Development.

The production of an accurate and realistic financial plan is fundamental to the whole strategic planning process, and as mentioned in the previous chapter, it is a task for which a large majority of owner-managers are not suitably equipped. The production of budgetary plans and cash flow forecasts is frequently seen as an unpleasant chore, an annual burden that detracts from the mainstream running of the business, and adds nothing measurable in terms of profit or productivity. This attitude leads to the tendency to get it over with as quickly as possible, and to use short cuts, rounded figures and approximations to save time and effort. In the back of the mind lies the view that attention to fine detail and accuracy is pointless when the actual income and expenditure figures will invariably differ right from day one.

Once again, this is where we see the need for another culture shift and change of attitude on the part of the owner-manager. When expansion or diversification is being considered, then it is critically important to be as detailed and accurate as possible in formulating the financial plans for the business. Omissions or underestimates can leave the business with insufficient working capital that might restrict the rate of expansion that can be achieved. The rounding-up of cost forecasts and the building-in of contingency sums might provide a safety margin, but if the budgetary plan is to provide the basis for variance analysis between planned and actual costs, those safety margins will distort and invalidate the comparison. Rounding-up of sales forecasts can be even more disastrous when revenue projections are based on overambitious figures. Obviously, some figures must be based on a best guess if no historical data are available. For example, it is hard precisely to estimate the annual running and maintenance of costs of vehicles, but in such cases the obvious tactic is to isolate such items and enter them in a separate line in the forecast, so that they can be monitored.

The culture shift that is needed for effective financial planning is the appreciation of the importance of accuracy and attention to detail during the stages of preparing the financial plans. If the owner-manager remains reluctant to get directly involved in preparing the plans, then it will be necessary to pay or employ a suitably skilled person to do the job, and to be prepared to give them sufficient co-operation, time and information for them to achieve the necessary accuracy. This is not simply a task that can be delegated to the first available employee who has a bit of spare time, or who can use a calculator quite well.

## The planning process

Figure 10.1 outlines the process that is involved in formulating the financial plan, and in practice, it follows the chapter patterns in this book. The market research process will have identified opportunities in the market, the marketing and sales plans will have identified the strategy for achieving the market share and forecasting the sales volumes and revenues, and the costs involved in doing so. The sales volumes will give the production side of the business information about the volume of output needed so that production and distribution costs can be identified. The output targets will also determine whether or not current capacity is adequate, and what additional resources are required. These may be capital items such as the purchase and installation of new production machines, staff training for these, new delivery vehicles, or the research and development of new product lines. Alternatively, they may be paid for out of the revenue budget (the working capital), such as raw materials and the wages of staff to operate the new machinery. The phasing of the expansion and the key aspects of its implementation, such as the sales and promotion activities, and the installation of additional production capacity, will be reflected in the budgetary plan for the business, that will incorporate both the revenue and capital budgets. That will in turn enable the production of a cash flow forecast which will identify any cash flow problems, i.e. where there is a deficit in working capital that must either be bridged by short-term borrowing such as an overdraft, or if the gap is substantial, by an injection of funds from such as additional capital or a bank loan. That, together with the capital budget items, will determine the total amount of longer-term borrowing and/or additional equity that the business requires, and the budgetary plan will have identified the points in time when the funding would be needed. All that remains is for the decisions to be made by the owner-managers about suitable types of funding and the sources of these.

The most appropriate form of borrowing will be determined by a number of factors:

- The purpose for which the funds are required, e.g. whether it is to increase working capital, or to acquire a vehicle or an item of capital equipment. For the former, some form of short-term funding would be most appropriate, whereas to finance the purchase of plant and equipment, longer-term finance might be better, e.g. leasing, hire purchase or a bank loan.

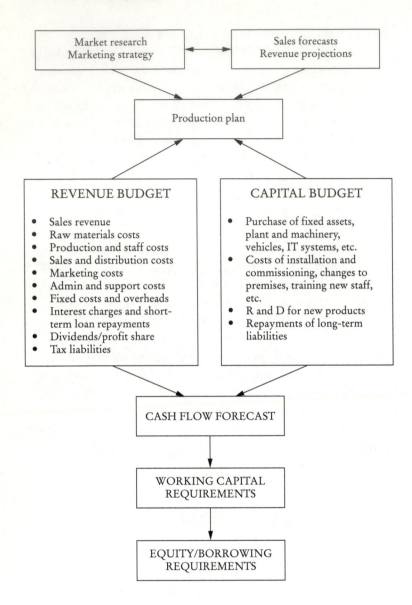

*Figure 10.1* Formulating the financial plan

- The size of the borrowing requirement. Most bankers will only lend against security. A personal guarantee might be acceptable to cover a loan of a few thousand pounds, but for a more substantial sum, the loan will need to be secured by a legal charge on some property or other tangible asset. Borrowing small sums of money can also be quite expensive in that interest rates tend to be high for smaller sums, but reduce as the size of the loan increases. Also, with small loans, the initial set-up fees charged by banks or lenders form a larger proportion of the total cost.

- The availability of security or collateral. Bankers will rarely lend against the full equity value of property, and will seldom offer to lend more than 80 per cent of the equity value, on the grounds that if property values fall, the borrower may be in a negative-equity situation. In fact, 50 per cent is a more realistic figure for some high street banks, especially when the borrower is the owner-manager of a newly established small business. If the net equity value of your home is £50k, then you may only be able to borrow £25k to £30k against it. An alternative is to offer the bank a Fixed and Floating Charge against the book debts and assets of the business. This is an option for limited companies that own some measurable and tangible fixed assets, whereby a legal charge is registered against the company by the lender with the Registrar of Companies. In the event of insolvency, it gives the lender first call on all of the fixed assets of the business (the Fixed Charge) and on any current assets of the business including the debtors (the Floating Charge).

- The period over which repayment will be made. Short-term borrowing tends to incur higher rates of interest, often 5 per cent above the base lending rate, whereas the interest rate is usually lower when spread over a longer period, e.g. 2 or 3 per cent over base rate. Some forms of finance also have maximum repayment periods, such as commercial mortgages, or repayment periods that are linked to the size of the borrowing and the potential life-time of the asset, as in the case of car loans.

- The rate of repayments that the borrower can afford. The important question when assessing funding options is 'Can my business afford to make the required regular payments from its current or forecast levels of profit?' If not, then the whole viability of any expansion plans must be questioned, or the owner-manager must look towards raising more equity (e.g. by perhaps selling a share of the business), or finding some cheaper, longer-term finance, perhaps another lender who will consider lower repayments spread over a longer period.

In practice, one form of borrowing alone will not normally satisfy the needs of a growing business, and will probably not be the most cost-effective. The optimum borrowing pattern may combine several types of funding possibly obtained from different sources, and combining both long-term and short-term facilities. For example, the bulk of the expansion costs might be financed by means of a five- or ten-year bank loan, with seasonal fluctuations in sales revenue covered by an over-draft arrangement, production machinery financed by hire purchase, vehicles on lease, and with the use of factoring to improve cash flow.

This is really most appropriate to plug gaps in working capital requirements, and several options are available:

***Short-term borrow-ing***

- Overdrafts are intended to be a short-term form of borrowing, available to cover temporary periods when cash flow may be poor, for example during the winter months in the holiday trade. Bank overdrafts are normally approved for up to one year, with the original approval and any subsequent re-approval incurring an arrangement fee, typically £50 or a minimum of 1 per cent of the approved overdraft, whichever is the greater. Interest rates are usually quite high, but there again, interest is only charged when the overdraft facility is in use. The important thing to remember is that if you find that you need a permanent overdraft, then you do not need an overdraft at all, you really need a loan.

- Unsecured loans – unless you have a long-standing and proven track record, obtaining an unsecured business loan from a bank, for anything but a small sum over a very short period, is virtually impossible. Loans from close friends or relatives might be available, but even if these are arranged on an unsecured basis, it is worthwhile formalizing the terms and conditions of the loan in writing, to protect both lender and borrower.

- Short-term bank loans would be more suitable, for example, when a business is expanding and expects to have a consistent cash shortfall for perhaps the first twelve months of the expansion period. In this case, the loan would need to be sufficiently large to cover the anticipated shortfall (plus a bit in reserve) and the loan repayments during the period of expected shortfall. Such a loan would probably be repayable over twenty-four to thirty-six months, and would prove a cheaper alternative to an overdraft facility because of the lower rates of interest.

- Factoring or Invoice Discounting involves the management of the firm's sales ledger by an outside organization, typically the factoring division of a lending bank. Initially, all of the customers of the business, and all subsequent new customers, are given a very tight and careful credit check. Once approved, the factoring company guarantees to pay the business a fixed percentage (e.g. up to 80 per cent) of the value of every invoice within fourteen days of the issue of the invoice. The balance of the debt (less a factoring charge) is paid to the business once the customer has settled the debt. Factoring can be excellent

155

for cash flow, but the factoring companies are very strict and can be heavy-handed in dealing with customers, which can result in the loss of trade. There is also usually a minimum turnover requirement of £250k, and the business will normally be expected to sign a long-term contract, typically five years, which can be hard and expensive to get out of. Invoice discounting works in a similar fashion, but in this case, the sales ledger is controlled by the company itself, with advances of up to 80 per cent being made against specific invoices. The company repays the advance when the debt is collected, and interest is charged at between 2 and 5 per cent over normal commercial rates. This is almost like an overdraft facility, but with lower interest rates for the long-term contractual commitment.

## Long-term finance

Unless the owner-managers have access to substantial financial resources through family or personal connections, then the expansion programme will almost certainly have to be funded by some form of borrowing. There are various options available:

- Equity or capital. From the owner-manager's viewpoint, the best form of long-term funding is equity, because it does not incur interest charges, and dividends or profit shares are only paid out when the business makes a trading profit, and not always then if the owners want to use the money for expansion. Equity can take the form of money invested in the business by the owners, or as reserves arising from retained profits from trading. Raising capital for expansion can be hard for owners of small firms unless they have rich relatives or plenty of cash slopping around. The easiest option is to utilize any equity in the family home or other property, e.g. by means of a second mortgage. However, this still has to be funded, which usually means that the owner-manager has to draw extra money (which is taxable) from the business to meet the mortgage payments. An alternative is to sell part of the business to a third party, but that can result in loss of control or interference with the way in which the business is managed, and finding potential investors can be quite hard.

- Venture Capital is one source of extra equity that can be achieved without losing control of the business. Venture Capital organizations are specialist companies whose primary activity is to invest in new businesses and unquoted companies to help them expand and grow. Investments can take the form of loans or minority shareholdings, but typically, Venture Capitalists are usually only interested in investing sums exceeding £500k. They generally seek investments that offer them potentially high returns (20–40 per cent of capital investment) over several years from dividends and capital growth to justify the investment risks that they take. They frequently seek boardroom representation, they require regular and detailed reports and information, and will normally expect the business in which they have invested to buy out their share after a specified period of time. Venture Capital companies can provide the levels of investment that might otherwise only be obtainable via the Stock Exchange, but without the massive cost of achieving Stock Exchange listing. They also impose structure and regulation on company affairs, and can provide valuable management expertise. On the negative side, they can limit the owners' ability to make decisions, their expectations are high, and the owner loses a good deal of strategic control over the business. The owner must also pay for the initial legal and accountancy charges to facilitate the capital injection. On balance, they do offer a great opportunity to finance the expansion of small firms in high-growth industrial sectors.

- Medium- to long-term loans from banks. High street banks will make medium- and long-term loans to businesses, typically over five to ten years, on a secured basis, and with interest rates around 3 per cent over the base lending rate (or 5 per cent for a new business without a trading record). Beyond that period, the loan is more likely to be treated as a mortgage, being secured by a specific fixed asset belonging to the business or one of its proprietors. Again, arrangement fees are charged and there may be some solicitors' costs incurred in setting up legal charges on property.

- Loans from merchant banks. It is often said that it is easier for a business to borrow £10 million than just £10 000. Most of the merchant banks and financial institutions that specialize in providing business finance have little interest in setting up long-term loans of less than £250k, as the time and effort involved do not justify the potential profit. This policy does leave small firms very much at the behest of the high street banks, as the bigger institutions have no interest in lending to them, so this type of borrowing is really best suited to companies that are already well established and which are looking for six-figure sums to finance substantial growth. Loans from merchant banks are invariably secured, if not by property or assets, then by a debenture, probably supplemented with directors' guarantees. Interest and capital repayments are made monthly or quarterly, with interest rates set at prearranged levels. Arranging the loans will incur legal costs, and larger loans can take several months to negotiate and set up.

- Flotation on the Stock Exchange or Alternative Investment Market (AIM) can be a very expensive process, and is generally regarded as not being justified unless the floating company intends to raise at least £5 million. The company has to prove that it can meet specific accounting, operational and capitalization standards in order to find a merchant bank willing to underwrite the flotation (i.e. to buy up all of the surplus shares if no one else likes the look of them). Once listed, its shares can be sold to the public, and the capital raised can be used for expansion. Flotation has become very popular amongst small high-tech and e-commerce businesses (the so-called dot-coms), but as a result of a number of failures, investors are becoming increasingly wary about buying shares in these types of business. Flotation also places the business under public scrutiny and reduces the autonomy and control of the owner-manager, who becomes an employee accountable to the shareholders.

- Debentures are a special type of fixed-term loan, often guaranteed by a charge on the assets of the business, and sometimes linked to an option to convert into share capital. They differ from conventional loans in that, during the lifetime of the loan, only interest is paid. The capital sum does not fall due for repayment until the period of the loan expires, when it must be repaid in full. Interest rates are agreed at the start of the term either at a fixed level or linked to commercial lending rates, with a minimum specified level. Debentures will often be arranged between one company and another, or by financial institutions, particularly to assist with expansion of a business. They can therefore be particularly useful and attractive to small firms that are looking to expand. How do you find another firm that might be willing to loan the money? Well, look first to your own suppliers and customers. It may be that you have a supplier that is fairly large and well established that might welcome the opportunity of a fairly safe and secured investment that would both consolidate its relationship with one of its customers, and at the same time increase its sales to that customer. Similarly, if you have a large customer that depends on your supplies, a debenture can cement the relationship, guaranteeing both their source of supply (possibly on favourable terms) and a proportion of your sales.

- Convertible loan stock takes the form of an option to buy shares in a company, which is issued against loans,

typically from financial institutions or investment companies. The company that issues the shares receives a loan,
usually at quite low interest rates, with no capital repayments until the settlement date, and with the interest being
paid out of pre-tax earnings, so this amounts to a very
cheap form of finance. The lending company, as well as
receiving interest on the loan, has an option at the end
of the loan period. If the borrowing company's shares
have performed poorly, the loan can be repaid in full and
return the share option. Alternatively, if the shares have
increased in value in the meantime, the lender can exer-
cise its right to buy them at the original price in lieu of
repayment of the loan (i.e. 'convert' the loan into shares)
and sell them for a capital profit. How does this fit in
with the expansion needs of small firms, particularly if,
as is highly likely, their shares are not publicly quoted?
Irrespective of a lack of Stock Exchange listing, there is
nothing to stop a small company from selling its shares
privately, so as with the debentures, look towards your
supply chain for potential financiers or investors.

- The availability of grants to assist with business expansion can depend largely on the location of the business.
Some relocation grants are available for businesses starting
up or moving to development areas, particularly in more
remote rural areas, e.g. in Wales. Local authorities in urban
redevelopment areas often have access to European Social
Fund monies, which are sometimes issued in grant form
to assist small firms. Local councils or chambers of
commerce can often advise on the availability of these, as
they will differ from area to area. Grants to subsidize
training for employees can also be obtained from some
local authority economic development units, and from
most Business Links (the public face of the government's
Small Business Service) or Enterprise Agencies, particularly if your business is working towards Investors in
People status. Regional Enterprise Grants may be available to assist with capital projects in some areas, providing

up to 15 per cent of the cost (maximum cost £15 000), and the Rural Development Commission can provide grants to help with the cost of converting rural buildings for business purposes.

- Hire purchase is usually used to buy a fixed asset such as a vehicle or an item of plant or machinery. Under a hire purchase agreement, a business would typically pay 20–25 per cent of the cost of the asset plus the full VAT sum up front, with the hire purchase company financing the balance. The VAT is claimed back at the next quarter, and fixed monthly payments are then made over a specific period of time, perhaps three to five years, at the end of which the asset belongs to the business. In case of default on monthly payments, the hire purchase finance company, which still technically owns the asset until the final payment is made, can recover and sell the asset. If the business has already paid at least two-thirds of the money due, then recovery will require a Court Order. Hire purchase is useful to a business that wants to show the fixed asset on its balance sheet, but being a capital purchase, capital allowance taxation rules apply. For a small firm that wants to expand and needs to buy fixed assets, hire purchase can provide a useful alternative to bank loans as the asset that is bought secures the finance, although in the case of limited companies, a director's guarantee is usually requested. If the owner-manager only has limited collateral to secure a bank loan, then the use of hire purchase can avoid tying up that security and leave it free for other purposes. The interest payable on hire purchase is normally higher than that incurred in a bank loan, but rates do vary between finance companies, and it pays to shop around.

- Leasing or contract hire. Whereas with hire purchase the asset eventually becomes the property of the business, in the case of lease hire or contract hire the transfer of ownership does not occur. Under a leasing contract the business simply makes regular monthly payments to the leasing company over the duration of the contract, and has the use of the asset during that time. Leasing is cheap and easy to set up, usually requiring an up-front deposit of only three months' payments, with VAT being charged on each payment. It is good for cash flow and tax-effective, as all payments count as a business expense; however, as the ownership of the asset never changes hands, it cannot be shown as a fixed asset in the firm's balance sheet.

- Commercial mortgages are used to buy business premises or to expand premises that are already owned. A commercial mortgage arranged through a bank, insurance company or financial institution is basically the same as a mortgage used to buy a private home. It would normally be repaid over ten to fifteen years, as opposed to the typical twenty-five-year repayment period for a domestic mortgage. Commercial mortgages for licensed premises can also be obtained from some of the regional and national breweries, linked to a contract to buy their products (a barrellage loan). For owner-managers in the pub trade, or hotel and tourism industries, these arrangements can be useful if the target for expansion involves acquiring multiple outlets.

- The Loan Guarantee Scheme (LGS) was introduced by the government in the early 1980s to encourage banks to lend to new and small firms whose proprietors could not offer any conventional security. The idea was that the government, in return for a percentage charge, would guarantee up to 85 per cent of the value of the loan. The banks, in return for a higher rate of loan interest, would stand the risk of the other 15 per cent. Loan guarantees can still be found, but the scheme as a whole is generally viewed as a failure. Apart from the high cost of interest and fees, banks simply do not like to risk lending even as little as 15 or 20 per cent to a small business on an unsecured basis, and so were only willing to advance money to established firms with a proven track record. Home-owning applicants were told that as they had potential security, the LGS was inappropriate. Applicants with no assets were asked why the bank should risk backing them, when they had nothing at risk themselves. Loans are available for anything between £5000 and £250 000 over two to ten years, and for most business purposes (although not for licensed premises), but they must not be used to replace existing finance. The idea sounds very attractive to owner-managers as a low-risk means of raising money for expansion, but the loans can prove to be a very expensive form of borrowing. Interest rates are high, often about 5 per cent over base rate, to reflect the risk that the banks are sharing. On top of this, there is a DTI premium of 3 per cent for the government's guarantee, and arrangement fees have to be paid at the outset. The loans can also take time to set up, as if they exceed £30 000 they need both bank and government approval, but below that figure the banks can approve them quite quickly.

In summary, if the strategic objectives for expansion are to be achieved, the owner-manager must plan the finances of the business to ensure that:

- The business has sufficient cash flow and liquidity to finance the growth without the risk of over-trading. Do not leave the business short of working capital at the time when it is needed most.

- The amount of funding is sufficient to do the job properly, i.e. to enable the business to achieve the desired level of expansion smoothly and without interruption. Build a contingency sum or safety margin into your figures, as you will invariably need it at some point.

- The terms of any borrowing (interest rates, etc.) are commercially competitive so as not adversely to affect

163

profit margins. Do not be afraid to challenge the rates offered by potential lenders. Shop around and negotiate. The banks need your business as much as you need their money.

- The ratio of borrowing to security is not unfavourable. The banks might like twice as much security as the sum advanced, but this could limit any further borrowing at a later date. In addition, the amount of security that is provided by the owner-manager's private resources should not be so large that it constitutes an unacceptable risk or causes personal stress or family disputes. Running a business is stressful enough without adding to the problem.

- The repayment terms of any borrowing are within the capacity of the business, and do not overstretch it. Any borrowing must be affordable otherwise it will eat into working capital and cause cash flow problems.

- The types of funding are appropriate to purposes for which they are sought, e.g. the use of overdrafts for short-term financing only, or the use of hire purchase to buy machinery or vehicles.

- The sources of finance meet both the needs of the business and the aspirations of the owner-manager in terms of ownership and control. For example, do not be forced into relinquishing control of the business by selling shares in order to raise money.

- Finally, make sure that you have an accounting system that enables you to keep full control of the finances of the business, and gives you the information you need, when you need it.

# Chapter 11 Implementing
Chapter 11 Chapter 11 the strategic
plan

So far, we have decided on the direction in which the business will be going, researched the market and planned the sales and marketing activities, decided on the physical and staff resources that will be required and when and how they will be obtained, and finally, we have forecast the cash flow and capital funding requirements and what combination of finance will best match the needs of the business. Now all that remains is to put the different parts of the jigsaw together to complete the strategic plan, and of course actually to make it work, the problem here being that the implementation stage is probably the most critical of all, and the one that has the biggest propensity for problems to occur, particularly if the sequence and phasing of the implementation are not carefully planned and organized. Hopefully, the right decisions for the future of the business have already been made, but now comes the time to decide how to make those earlier decisions work together.

This chapter relates to Units D1, D3 and D4 of the Revised Business Development Standards, which involve preparing an action plan for the expansion of the business, preparing for and implementing change, and gathering information to monitor the process and make critical decisions as and when needed.

**The chicken and egg situation**

Obviously, before you can start implementing the changes to your business, you need to have the necessary finances in place, but once the money is available and ready for use, where do you start? Do you ensure that all of your capital investment activities are in place to ensure that you have full production capacity before commencing the marketing? This would incur the risk of having the machinery standing idle or only working at half-capacity whilst sales are built up, and draining your working capital in the process. Alternatively, do you start your marketing early while the extra capacity is being installed, and then risk making your customers wait for delivery? This would not be a particularly good advertisement for your business and might well risk the loss of your new-found custom? An engineering or manufacturing firm would probably have no choice but to install the plant before starting the sales push, as the commissioning of new production systems inevitably involves teething problems that must be sorted if the firm's quality standards and reputation are not to suffer. A wholesale or retail business may need to focus on the provision of adequate space or distribution capacity before the sales push, but may be able to build up its stock levels in line with growing demand. And a service business based around people-skills might adopt an incremental approach to implementation, by phasing its recruitment or training and development of new staff to be achieved slightly ahead of its anticipated new custom. This allows the new people to grow into the job with minimal risk to the firm's quality and reputation, and ensures that the financial outlay is quickly recovered, minimizing working capital requirements and potential cash flow problems.

Of course, the perfect scenario would be to achieve a seamless transition from the current level of activity to operating at the new increased capacity. However, any transition from a small to a larger organization, or any major diversification of activities, requires the careful management of two inherently incompatible media – People and Change – and the fact remains that people simply do not like change in their lives!

## Change manage- ment

This topic could fill a book in its own right, but most owner-managers would probably consider themselves too busy to read it anyway, so we will consider some of the key factors involved in the subject. The implementation of strategic objectives is usually a difficult process because it almost certainly requires significant changes to occur in the business, and any form of change is a potential source of problems or conflict. Fortunately, in smaller organizations, the extent of the changes that are needed is likely to be less, or of less impact, than would be the case in a big company. Furthermore, the change process is often easier because of the more open and direct lines of communication that normally exist between the people within the business. Similarly, in a small firm, the critical, but often routine, functions or systems that are important to the running of the business tend to be under the close or direct control of the owner-manager. This can be important to the implementation of the new strategies, as any problems that arise within these systems during the change process tend to be noticed more quickly. On the other hand, if the owner-manager does get distracted and fails to monitor progress, in a small firm there may be no other person around to spot the problems that are occurring.

Before the owner-manager can think about implementing proposals for expansion or diversification, he or she needs to consider the impact of those proposals on the other people involved in the business, and to gain a perception of their perspectives. For most mortals, change provokes feelings of uncertainty, uncertainty creates fear and apprehension, fear incites negative attitudes and dissension, and before you know it, the whole workforce has become totally demotivated and uncooperative, and why did this happen? All because you probably did not take enough time and effort right from the start to tell them what was going on, and how it would or would not affect them!

The effective management of change is a skill most people learn by default or in retrospect, and it is a skill that owner-managers tend to be especially insensitive about and particularly poor at handling. This is usually because the sole focus of their attention is on what they want the business to achieve, and not on how to get the other stakeholders around them to help them in the process. This constitutes yet another aspect of the culture shift that must be made by the owner-manager before embarking on strategic development of the business, by moving away from 'what I want the business to do' towards 'what we can achieve in the business'.

So, the main points that need to be considered when making changes are:

- Keep your staff informed of what is happening right from the start. You do not have to tell them every single graphic detail, but by outlining the main changes that will occur you can avoid the sort of speculation and rumour that creates fear and demotivation. Think back to how you have felt in the past when changes were going on around you, and you might then just appreciate their perspective.

- Sell the benefits and advantages of the proposals to your staff. If they are convinced or at least positive about the purpose of the changes, you will be more likely to gain their full support and co-operation. Play down the aspects of disruption as being just issues of short-term inconvenience, and promote the prospects of secure employment and development opportunities that the long-term profitability of the business would confer. The object of this is to get your staff to take ownership of the changes, because if they do so, then the whole change process will be easier and smoother to achieve.

- Listen carefully to their concerns and objections to get an insight into their perceptions of the change, and respond positively to these. Give them regular opportunities to air their views and specific channels to do so, perhaps a short weekly feedback meeting with representatives or supervisors. This again contributes towards the ownership of the changes, and to breaking down any barriers that might stand between them and what you want to achieve.

- Consult them about details of the implementation, as not only does this help with the ownership of change, it will almost certainly throw up some useful or practical ideas that you have overlooked, that could make the implementation easier. You may be the owner-manager but you do not have a monopoly on good ideas.

- At the end of the process, thank them for their co-operation, and if it has been a success, perhaps make a special occasion out of doing so. You night need their co-operation again in the future.

## Getting the systems right

In the previous section, there was a brief reference to the essential functions or systems that are critical to the operation of the business. If the strategic objectives of the business are to be successfully implemented, then first, it is critical to identify the systems that will need to be in place in order to achieve them. The key systems will typically be those that actively contribute towards the primary goals or profitability of the business. For example, the production functions that manufacture goods for sale, the people systems in service industries that produce services to customers, and the sales and marketing activities that sell those goods or services to the customers. This is all about having the right resources in place to achieve the objectives. Are the current systems adequate to cope with expansion or diversification? Is there sufficient manufacturing capacity, and do we have the skilled staff to run the machines? Do we have the trained and experienced staff to provide an increased level of services? Have we got the sales and marketing structure in place to create the demand that will take up the newly created capacity? Without these key systems in place, the strategic development of the business will not work, which is precisely why they must be right before we can get started.

The second stage is to ensure that the support systems are in place. These are the functions that enable the key systems to operate smoothly, such as the purchasing, stores, administration and distribution functions, not forgetting the management systems to organize and co-ordinate these. Again, if the current support systems are unable to cope with the planned growth, then supplementary or new resources will need to be installed or developed alongside, or preferably in advance of, the extra demand and output created by the key systems. For example, a doubling of output or sales may create a proportionate increase in the administration system, to ensure that invoices go out on time, and that customers pay their bills promptly. This may simply involve employing an extra administrative assistant, but equally it might mean upgrading the computerized accounting systems and training staff to operate it. The former can be achieved in a few days, but the latter might take weeks or months to become fully operational.

The third stage is to ensure that adequate monitoring and control systems are in place, both to monitor the expansion of old or the implementation of new systems, and to monitor the efficacy of the whole strategic process and its component parts. Lasher (1999, p. 135) remarks that strategic control is the same as any other form of control, it just has more variables than most. This means that in order to be in control of those variables, the monitoring process needs to be made that much tighter. This can be achieved by increasing the level and extent at which each monitoring process operates, perhaps by increasing the frequency of monitoring, or by scrutinizing each aspect in more detail. Alternatively, it could be achieved by increasing the actual number and range of monitoring processes that are in use. This would mean, for example, that the planning and review cycle illustrated in Figure 11.1 might be applied to each of the individual functions and systems that contribute towards the strategic implementation, as well as to the process as a whole. The vital part of the loop is the feedback process that must occur after each evaluation, in order to facilitate the planning of the next stage or activity. Without the feedback to

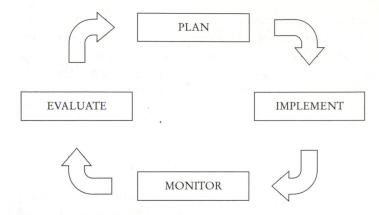

*Figure 11.1*   The planning and review cycle

close the loop, any essential changes or modifications that are necessary to make the plans work are at risk of being overlooked, and minor problems may be exacerbated, or may grow into expensive major problems.

## Critical events and stages of implementation

In order to implement both the key systems and support systems, it will be necessary to produce an action plan which identifies the critical dates by which each one of these systems must be in place. This is effectively the project planning process, that will determine the start dates and completion targets for the introduction of expansion of each system. In a small service business, this may just comprise a series of dates by which new staff must be recruited and trained for their new roles, and the schedule of advertising and promotion activities. In an engineering or manufacturing firm, it may entail the employment of a project planning consultant armed with flow charts and critical path analyses. This person would ensure that each part of the new systems is installed in the right sequence and within its own deadline, as any disruption to the timetable might be critical to the installation of subsequent parts of the system. The action plan should be regarded as a means to an end, as

171

opposed to something that, once set, cannot be changed. Although it sets the guidelines and targets for the process, it must be flexible enough to account for, and respond to, any factors that are beyond the control of the process. The project planning procedures must be, like the workings of each of the systems, subject to the same planning and review cycle if they are to function efficiently.

It is also important, when preparing plans for implementation and subsequently reviewing progress, to compare the dates and details with the other key plans of the business, i.e. the budgetary plans and cash flow forecasts. In fact, some aspects of the budgetary plans, such as the staged acquisition or release of funds, might be the factors that precipitate the next stages of implementation. Any interruption or delays in the implementation could have a major impact on the sales revenue and working capital situation if revenue is not going to be received when expected, particularly when expenditure is still ongoing. Delays are highly likely to increase overall costs and this could widen any potential cash flow deficit. It is one of the Universal Laws of Nature (and business) that, when managing a new project, whatever might conceivably go wrong will go wrong, and usually at the worst possible time, or when spare cash is at a minimum. It pays therefore to have a contingency plan in case of emergencies. Right from the early planning stages it is good practice to examine each phase or aspect of the project and to ask oneself (and preferably someone else with an objective viewpoint) what could possibly go wrong. List all of the possibilities, and perhaps grade them according to their relative probabilities, and then ask yourself how you would need to respond to each one if it occurred individually, or in combination with others. What impact would they each have on progress? What delays might be involved? And of course, what would be the cost implications? It also pays to build some slack into the time scale of the project to allow for delay, and ideally a contingency sum or safety margin into the budget to prepare for the expense those delays incur.

**Refer back to the strategic objectives**

The most critical factor of all to remember is that, throughout the whole process of implementing the business development strategy, it is imperative that you keep referring back to the strategic objectives. This is to ensure that whatever you are doing by way of implementation will be compatible with, and will complement, those objectives. It is very easy to get side-tracked during the implementation stage, perhaps by spotting and pursuing an opportunity that seems like a good idea and that might improve short-term profit, but which will ultimately detract from your longer-term objectives. The best way or ensuring compliance with your main objectives is to build it in as a matter of regular practice, at the evaluation stage within the planning and review cycle. This means that as part of the evaluation you automatically check that the information and outcomes derived from the monitoring activities are compatible with your overall business development strategy and/or its component parts.

Finally, once the implementation of your strategy is complete, that is when you must start to apply the monitoring and review process to the strategy as a whole, to ensure that it continues to work for you, to identify at an early stage any actions that are needed to keep it on track, or any changes that are required to make it work better for you. Strategic planning, whether it is for a large or small business, is an ongoing process, and the strategic plan should be a living document to reflect that situation, not just a heap of papers stranded in the bottom of the filing tray. Above all, do not fall back into the old habits of the pre-culture shift days, where the strategic issues are subsumed by the everyday operational aspects of running the business.

*Reference*

Lasher, W. (1999). *Strategic Thinking for Smaller Businesses and Divisions*. Blackwell.

*Further reading*

Drummond, G. and Ensor, J. (1999). *Strategic Marketing Planning and Control*, Chapter 12. Butterworth-Heinemann.
Lasher, W. (1999). *Strategic Thinking for Smaller Businesses and Divisions*, Chapter 8. Blackwell.

In Chapter 8, we looked briefly at the organizational skills needed by owner-managers, the need to be able to organize others, to organize their own time and prioritize their work, and to be able to delegate work to others. We also mentioned the broad range of business skills that owner-managers need, especially in the early stages of the business. However, when it comes to self-development, owner-managers are often their own worst enemies, frequently putting the short-term needs and pressures of work ahead of the need to enhance their own management capabilities and competence. There is also a core of owner-managers who are blind to their own short-comings and do not even recognize that there is a need for self-development for themselves or their staff. Unit A3 of the Revised Business Development Standards requires owner-managers to review and evaluate their own personal skills, and particularly those that will be needed to manage an expanding business.

## Barriers to training uptake by small firms

In the early stages of a business when money is tight, owner-managers will pay for staff to attend short (and preferably inexpensive) courses to acquire essential skills, but staff development in general tends to be kept to the affordable minimum. This is because it is regarded as being either not absolutely essential or a necessary evil which just adds to overhead costs and takes up valuable working time.

175

Much research has been carried out into the barriers that affect the uptake of training in small firms, and the findings from these reveal that owner-managers are looking for four key factors when they consider training or development:

- Courses must be available at convenient times, i.e. outside of the main working week. Neither the owner-managers nor their staff can be spared from work to attend training during core working hours. This may be due to the sheer pressure of work or to the lack of cover for key staff who are absent. Unfortunately, the bulk of available training opportunities tend to be offered within that same core of working hours, and the immediate demands of work inevitably take priority.

- Courses must be reasonably priced. The high cost of conventional accredited management development programmes normally runs into hundreds of pounds, at lower levels, and thousands for higher level programmes, DMS, MBA, etc. These prices are simply unaffordable to many new and developing firms, that may only be making small profits in the early stages, and that need to reinvest those profits to keep the business going.

- Programmes must offer a rapid and measurable payback on the investment. The substantial time commitment involved in attending conventional training courses that often span one or two academic years is unattractive to small firms who want to be able to apply the learning immediately, and see corresponding quick results.

- Training must be available locally, where it can be accessed quickly and easily without wasting core working time travelling around the countryside, when working time is at a premium. One of the other interesting side issues of the research was that a large proportion of owner-managers were often totally unaware of just what useful business and management training was available in their locality. This was partly because they had not looked around properly, but largely because of inadequate or low levels of marketing by the training providers, especially local colleges that tend to target larger organizations for business and management training.

As the firms start to grow, these old attitudes and inhibitions still pervade, and new management skills are introduced only when really required. It seems as if there is some unspecified and unidentifiable critical mass, beneath which staff development is treated as a necessary expense, but once that mass or size is reached, the owner-managers seem to become enlightened and start to welcome the development. Perhaps this occurs when other managers are brought on board, or perhaps it is due to a realization that staff training and development can be cheaper in the long term than recruiting skilled staff.

## Vocational training for owner-managers

Until recent years, the main part-time opportunities for management development comprised National Diplomas in Business Studies, or Certificates and Diplomas in Management at local colleges, or MBAs at university business schools. As stated above, these are both expensive and time consuming, but most important of all, having been designed to meet the needs of bigger national or international organizations, they tended to be largely irrelevant to the needs of small firms. The alternative that evolved in the early 1990s were the National Vocational Qualifications (NVQs) in Management at supervisory management, middle management and senior management levels, but again these were fundamentally geared towards the training needs of large firms. Their small-firm variant, the NVQ level 4 in Owner-Management, was only available as a full qualification, typically requiring a year of study, and involving significant costs and a substantial time commitment, just to basically prove that the candidate was competent to do what he or she was already doing.

This book has been written around the Revised SFEDI Vocational Standards for Business Development that are now

177

replacing the former NVQ4 in Owner-Management. Apart from being written in a much more user-friendly and plain English style, the new standards have been designed to be used in convenient bite-sized blocks or clusters of Units which are appropriate to the needs of the individual owner-manager at any particular point in time. So, for example, it is possible to take just the three Mandatory Units relating to the Business Health Check, A1, A2 and A3, which relate to the assessment of the performance of the business and its owner-managers to date. Alternatively, you could take several of the B Units (see Appendix for details) that relate to sales and marketing activities, or take some of the G Units concerning financial management. Using this modular approach, owner-managers can, if desired, work up to achieving a full NVQ4 qualification over a period of time, but at their own pace and convenience.

In the preface to this book, there was mention of the government's Small Business Service (SBS), which came into effect in April 2001, using the brand of Business Link, and offering co-ordinated one-stop services for small firms. One of the main objectives of SBS is to help co-ordinate the provision of development opportunities for small firms, this having previously been a very fragmented activity. One of the anticipated outcomes of SBS will hopefully be a change of emphasis from the former funding of whole qualifications towards the funding of modular-based programmes, to allow owner-managers to tap into the appropriate type of training as and when they really need it.

The most essential thing for anyone considering NVQs to appreciate is that NVQ programmes, whether delivered on a modular basis or as complete qualifications, are only as good as the added value they bring to the business. NVQs focus on the assessment of a person's competence to perform a task or role, by producing evidence of performance, and by demonstrating knowledge and understanding. Because of that, it is all

**Getting the best from NVQs**

too easy and tempting to achieve the qualification by looking back at past performance, which for the owner-manager might add little, apart from reflective analysis, to what he or she already knows. A good NVQ programme should comprise of both assessment opportunities and workshops for groups of candidates so that knowledge and competence can be developed as well as assessed. The optimum situation (i.e. the one that will give most added value to the candidates) is where the workshop sessions are used to develop the candidates' knowledge and understanding, and where they then go away to apply that new knowledge in the workplace. They then use the resulting outcomes to evidence their own competencies. What they are doing is learning about good or best practice, applying the learning, reflecting on its value or usefulness to the business, and using that reflection to develop themselves and for the future further benefit of the business. This is where the NVQ process really does begin to pay back the time and money invested. Returning to the heading of this chapter, it is one of the most assured ways in which owner-managers can develop the three key skills of organizing and prioritizing their own time, organizing others, and delegating responsibility to others.

**Back to the culture shift**

However, achieving competence in basic organization and planning skills is just the start of what it takes to be a successful entrepreneur. The rest is not so easy to achieve, because it requires an upward change of gear in attitude and thinking, i.e. the culture shift from operational to strategic thinking that was described in Chapter 1.

Bolton and Thompson (2000) have made a rather good and concise summary of ten characteristics, the 'Action Factors', that make the difference between an ordinary owner-manager and an entrepreneur:

- Entrepreneurs are individuals who make a difference to the environment in which they operate.

- Entrepreneurs are creative and innovative, and not afraid to try out new ideas.

- Entrepreneurs spot and exploit opportunities.

- Entrepreneurs find the resources required to spot and develop opportunities.

- Entrepreneurs are good networkers, utilizing existing contacts and constantly developing new ones.

- Entrepreneurs are determined in the face of adversity (sometimes even to the extent of being branded stubborn and obstinate!).

- Entrepreneurs manage risk and are prepared to take risks.

- Entrepreneurs have control of their businesses.

- Entrepreneurs put their customers first.

- Entrepreneurs create new capital rather than just using existing capital.

Finding all of these characteristics in one single person would probably be little short of a miracle, a million to one chance, but it is the one in a million entrepreneurs who are the household names: the Richard Bransons, the Alan Sugars, the Charles Fortes, the Walt Disneys and Bill Gates, to name just a few. If you cannot match them on all points, then why not try to emulate them on just a few key points. So, pick out two or three of the ten Bolton and Thompson characteristics that are particularly pertinent to your business. Put them in order of priority, and start to work on them in turn. Produce your own action plan for improving the way you do things, set specific and measurable targets, and check your progress regularly, and they might just make a difference to your success.

*Reference*

Bolton, B. and Thompson, J. (2000). *Entrepreneurs, Talent, Temperament, Technique*, p. 22. Butterworth-Heinemann.

# Appendix
Appendix
Appendix

## The revised SFEDI Standards for Business Development – summary of Units and Elements

The Revised Standards have been substantially changed from the originals as a result of extensive consultations with interested parties between 1999 and 2001, and the following Units and Elements are based on the latest draft available at the time of going to print. They incorporate three particular Units that have been incorporated from other Vocational Standards currently under development. Unit J4 has been imported from the Draft Personnel Unit P27, and Units K3 and K4 have been imported from the latest Learning and Development Draft Units L23 and L21.

The proposed full National Vocational Qualification will comprise the three Business Healthcheck Units which are all Mandatory, plus any three Optional Units taken from one or more of the Key Areas of Business Need.

**The Business Health-check (Mandatory A Units)**

A1  Review the business

● decide what you want for the business;

● find out what is affecting the business;

181

- check that the business is doing what you want it to do;
- decide which areas need improvement.

A2   Develop your plans for the business

- review the effectiveness of your marketing, sales, production, finances and staffing;
- produce an up-to-date plan for the business;
- plan your actions.

A3   Check your own management skills

- check your own performance;
- plan and develop your skills;
- find and use support and advice from others.

**Winning more business**

*Getting more sales – B Units*

B1   Plan how to improve your sales and marketing

- find out about the market for the business's products or services;
- plan your marketing;
- plan your sales;
- decide how you will judge the success of your marketing and sales.

B2   Improve your sales and marketing

- sell and market your products and services;
- make sure sales and marketing are helping the business.

**Key Areas of Business Need (Optional Units – select any three)**

B3   Explore markets abroad

- analyse markets abroad;
- plan how you will trade abroad;
- prepare to trade abroad;
- make sure that trading abroad benefits the business.

B4   Plan how to develop the business using the Internet

- produce an e-business plan;
- prepare to trade on the Internet;
- monitor the success of the website and e-trading activities.

B5   Sell products and services to customers

- identify the buying needs and interests of customers;
- promote the features and benefits of products and services to customers;
- help customers to overcome their queries and objections;
- agree terms and conditions and close sales.

B6   Negotiate sales

- prepare for sales negotiations;
- propose the terms of the sale;
- negotiate and agree the terms of the sale.

B7   Prepare and present sales proposals and quotations

- prepare proposals and quotations;
- present proposals and quotations.

*Getting new customers – C Units*

C1  Look after your customers

- check what your customers need from your business;
- decide how the business will meet customers' needs;
- meet your customers' needs.

C2  Improve your service to customers

- use customer feedback to plan improvements;
- change your service to customers;
- make sure your changes improve the quality of service customers receive.

C3  Solve customers' problems with the service given to the business

- identify problems;
- decide how to solve problems;
- solve problems.

C4  Improve relationships with your customers

- improve the way you communicate with your customers;
- balance the needs of your customers and the business;
- give your customers more than they expect.

## Running the business

*Getting the direction and controls right – D Units*

D1  Carry out your business plan

- prepare an action plan;

- make sure the plan is improving the business;
- review business performance against the plan.

D2 Improve the quality of your products and services

- review quality in the business;
- decide how to improve quality in the business;
- make sure the actions you take to improve quality help the business.

D3 Make changes to improve the business

- decide how the business can be improved;
- make sure the changes will benefit the business;
- plan how the changes will happen;
- make sure everybody understands the changes;
- make the changes.

D4 Take key decisions that affect the business

- gather information that may help you;
- identify things that may affect your decisions;
- take key decisions;
- keep others informed.

*Getting what you need – E Units*

E1 Get the right premises for the business

- review the business premises;
- choose premises for the business;
- agree the terms and conditions for the premises.

E2   Improve your use of equipment, tools and materials

- check you have the right equipment, tools and materials for the business;

- get equipment, tools and materials supplied;

- make sure that you continue to get the right equipment, tools and materials.

*Getting the most from IT – F Units*

F1   Develop a website for the business

- decide how the website will work;

- manage the technical development of the website.

F2   Communicate using IT

- choose and set up IT to communicate;

- send information using IT;

- receive information using IT;

- find electronically stored information when you need it.

F3   Choose and use computers and software

- choose and set up equipment and software;

- use equipment and resources properly;

- make sure IT systems are shut down correctly.

*Getting the most from money – G Units*

G1   Plan how to improve the finances of the business

- decide on the financial plan for the business;

- make sure that accounting systems are used effectively;

- provide financial forecasts;
- decide how capital should be invested.

G2  Make the most of finances in the business

- manage the cash flow of the business;
- increase the profitability of the business;
- develop working relationships with finance providers.

G3  Get finance for the business

- review different types of finance;
- decide who will provide finance for the business;
- agree terms and conditions for the finance;
- monitor how getting and servicing finance affects the business.

G4  Get customers to pay more quickly

- set up a credit control policy;
- put the credit control policy into practice;
- review the credit control policy.

## Getting the most from people in the business

*Delegating and managing your time – H Unit*

H1  Improve your time management and delegation skills

- review your own work activities;
- plan how to make better use of time and other people;
- delegate work to others effectively.

*Getting the right people – J Units*

J1    Review your staffing
- decide if the business has the right skills;
- plan your staffing.

J2    Deal with poor performance and handle staff complaints
- support staff who have problems that affect their work;
- discipline staff and handle staff complaints;
- dismiss staff whose work is unsatisfactory.

J3    Move staff to new roles or make them redundant
- plan how to move staff to new roles;
- move staff to new roles;
- make staff redundant.

J4    Recruit staff (Draft Personnel Unit – P27 – to be added when available)
- plan recruitment;
- advertise for jobs;
- select new staff.

*Getting more from staff and contractors – K Units*

K1    Make sure your staff can do their work
- monitor the work of your staff;
- improve your staff's skills.

K2   Get the right services or supplies from another business

- get services provided;
- deal with failures to meet the contract;
- agree variations to contracts;
- decide how to improve future contracts.

K3   Help your staff to learn (Learning and Development Draft Unit – L23 – Support and advise individual learners, to be added when available)

- help staff plan their learning;
- agree the support required;
- help staff to manage their own learning.

K4   Coach your staff (Learning and Development Draft Unit – L21 – Facilitate individual learning through coaching, to be added when available)

- coach staff;
- help your staff use their learning.

*Health and safety – L Units*

L1   Control risks to health and safety

- develop procedures to maintain a healthy and safe workplace;
- make sure your health and safety procedures are working.

L2   Conduct an assessment of risks in the workplace

- identify hazards in the workplace;
- assess the level of risk and recommend action;
- update your workplace assessment of risks.

# Index

Index
Index